An Ordinary Childhood

Poems and Stories

Eugene Coco

This book of poems and stories is lovingly dedicated to my cousin Emily Kaufman, whose guidance, motivation, and support were essential to its creation.

Table of Contents

Foreword

These pieces attempt to answer the most pressing and largely ignored questions of every life. How are we to love parents who, so broken themselves, love in ways that hurt bone-deep but still show the depth of their tenderness? How to reconcile within ourselves the disappointment of their darkest behaviors with a child's need to idealize them, coupled with the humanity you know is there? How not to become the worst of them, and take the very best of them, which they showed you so many times? And, most importantly, how to loosen the hold on you that they still have, so many years later, even though they're gone, and you mercifully see the totality of who they were?

These vignettes tell us how to aspire in that direction—to radically explore our feelings, both good and bad, in the hope of understanding. With kindness, forgiveness, and a touch of humor, Eugene takes us into an upbringing that all of us can in some measure identify with. If we let ourselves, the impact will be so moving that it might nudge us to be a little better, a little more accepting, and a lot more appreciative of the complexity of the many seemingly disparate elements that make us who we are.

— Michael Steinberg

Introduction

Recently, one of my friends told me that he was jealous that I could recall specific events in my life with such clarity that it was as if they were happening right now, even though some of them happened over fifty years ago. The events he alluded to have left an indelible mark on me, and have affected me in ways that are still making themselves known to me, even as I write this.

I was born in Bushwick, Brooklyn, in 1958, and moved to Borough Park with my mother at the age of six, when my parents divorced. Luckily for me they remained great friends, and up until my father's death in 1978, he would often come to my mother for comfort and advice when the pains of life became too much for him to handle. And my mother, who was brought up in a conservative Jewish household, somehow found the courage and resilience to overcome the intense sadness that had plagued her since she was an infant.

I am fortunate beyond words to have grown up with the greatest friends and family that any person could ever ask for, and that good fortune has continued to shine on me some sixty years later, as our mutual love for each other continues to grow and flourish. For without them, I would not have been able to survive as long as I have.

In writing this book of poems and prose poetry, it is my hope that people will in some way relate to the events that I have experienced throughout my childhood and adolescence, and learn from them so that they can realize that all of what we go through in growing up is essential in making us who we are. And above all, our past, as traumatic as it can be at times, will eventually make us better, more compassionate, and more understanding of ourselves and others, if we let it.

I am who I am

this is true;

but without you

who would I be?

Aisle Six

way before he let me try it by myself
which was some years later without his permission
I started watching him with great interest
my seat a little wooden bench
that I carried in from the living room
with both hands pressing it against my chest
squeezing in between the bathtub and the sink
though a little bit taller than four feet at the time
I had a great view of the whole procedure (my chin
resting on the cold white enamel of the bathroom sink)
which started with a basin full of hot water
in which a yellow washcloth was dropped
slowly sinking to the bottom
he would pick it up a few seconds later
a feat unto itself I thought
and wring it out just enough
so that not a single drop of water
would touch his pressed white t-shirt
then wrap his face inside it
until the bathroom mirror was completely steamed over
and after the first layer of shaving cream was wiped away
by the index finger of his left hand
he would survey every inch of his face
before applying the second layer
which was wiped away as well
only this time by a metal razor
sharpened by a leather strap
soft from years of many faces
and about this time
he would give me a wink
as if my concentration could ever waiver
then drain the sink
and from the bottom cabinet
after wiping clean any bit of shaving cream

that still remained
he would sprinkle in his left hand
some drops of Old Spice
and splash them on his face
in the process filling up my cupped hands as well
then in his hair
a bit more than the commercial said
squeeze some Brill Cream from a plastic tube,
just enough to keep his hair in place
and with a smile he would pick me up
and sling me over his shoulder
and bounce me all the way to his bedroom
where I'd sit on the edge of his bed
my feet dangling just above the floor
and watch him get dressed
the smell of Old Spice and Brill Cream
filling every inch of the world around me
and every once in a while
when it becomes just too much
that I forget his face
I'll walk to the corner drugstore
turn down aisle six
and splash a few drops of Old Spice on my face
squeeze some Brill Cream in my hair
close my eyes
and feel the cold white enamel
of the bathroom sink
on my chin again

A Great Plan

I came upon it by accident one day
after eating a box of Fig Newtons
and not making it to the bathroom in time
my mother following my trail
with a damp mop and wash cloth
shouting out instructions for me
to breathe through my nose
and lean over the toilet
she was sure the pain would go away
but it didn't, no matter how hard I prayed
what little was left of my stomach
I held tightly with both hands
squeezing out anything
that was left inside of me
hoping that it would help
but it only made things worse

afraid to lift up my head
and look at myself in the mirror
a few minutes later
I heard her hang up the phone
and after scraping off any remains
from the bathroom floor
she kissed the top of my head
helped me up, washed my face,
and said he'd be over soon
to drive us to the doctor

when I heard those words
the pain in my stomach
suddenly started to go away
and when he walked through the door
a little while later
it was almost completely gone

3

just the sight of him
could do that

feeling better than I had all week
I ran over to him
(still holding my stomach
just to make it look good)
and he asked me if I was ok
and I nodded yes
then he picked me up,
kissed me on the stomach
and we left our apartment
and walked down the street
to his car and I sat in the back
watching the both of them
sitting next to each other
just like it used to be

in the doctor's office
I jumped back when the nurse
pressed my stomach
(it really still did hurt a little bit)
"it's still a little tender," she said,
as she gave me a lollipop,
"but you'll be ok in a few hours"
and after filling the prescription
at the drugstore and buying me
a few comic books and a Matchbox Car
he took us out for lunch
both of them surprised
when I finished two slices of pizza,
a pretzel, and a bottle of Coke

a little while later he drove us
back to our apartment
and as he turned down our block
I thought maybe this time he would stay

at least for a little while
but he said he had to go to work
and suddenly I felt the pain
in my stomach come back
only this time
it wasn't because of the Fig Newtons

a week later I was waiting
for my mother to walk me to school
when suddenly I started missing him
so much I didn't know what to do
so I ran into the kitchen and emptied
a box of Fig Newtons in the garbage
then let out as loud a scream as I could
and by the time my mother made it to the bathroom
my head was in the toilet and she tried everything
but I kept on screaming until she had no choice
but to call him again because she had to go to work
and the doctor wasn't in until ten o'clock
and she didn't know what else to do

after he took me to the doctor
and filled another prescription
he spent the rest of the day with me
making banana sandwiches and playing checkers
while I sat on my bed and grabbed my stomach
every once in a while
just in case he suspected anything
but I think he knew what was going on
only he never told me

last Friday night we went out to dinner
then to some bar for a few drinks
and on the way home I stopped
to buy some rolls for breakfast
when I saw the last box of Fig Newtons
sitting there on the shelf of the store

I don't eat them anymore
but I bought them anyway
and when I got home
I emptied the box into the garbage
then sat around for a while missing them both
when suddenly I felt that old familiar pain in my stomach
and thought to myself what good is having a great plan
if you have no one to use it on anymore

Inheritance

He usually picked me up
after school on Fridays but
he called Thursday night
and said he would be a little late
and that he would pick me up outside
my apartment building around five o'clock

I was so excited to see him
that by four I went outside
to wait for him and waved
with both hands when his car
finally came around the corner
at about five-thirty

I grabbed my bag and walked
my bike over to him. it was
a Schwinn banana-seat bike
with high silver handlebars,
red reflector lights attached to
the front and back tires, brand
new baseball cards clipped to
the spokes with old clothespins
my mother gave me
and blue and white plastic streamers
that hung down from the handle-grips

I could tell right away
that something was wrong
because he wasn't smiling and
he didn't pick me up and swing
me over his shoulder like he
usually does when he sees me.
all he said was "let's get going
the traffic is really bad"

I put my bag in the back seat
of his car as he grabbed my bike
and tried to ram it into the trunk
of his blue 1972 Ford Custom sedan
only the newly polished handlebars
got stuck on the back fender and he
couldn't close the trunk so he
pulled the bike out and tried
twisting the handlebars but he still
couldn't get the bike to fit in the trunk
so he tried twisting the handlebars
the other way but that didn't work either
so he just started pushing on them
and pushing on them and pushing on
them until they started to bend the wrong way
then he tried to slam the trunk closed
but the handlebars kept sticking up
so he finally yanked the bike out
with one hand, slammed the trunk shut
with the other hand, and started smashing
the bike on the ground, kicking it a few times
and bending the frame in half before he picked it up
and threw it into the garbage cans that lined
the alleyway of my apartment building
all the time looking at me as if I did something wrong

I didn't know what to do
so I just stood there looking at
the broken red pieces of the reflectors
lying on the ground and watching the streamers
as they blew down the street. I thought
about running after them but I didn't want to
make him any madder than he already was
so I just got in the front seat of his car,
rolled down the window, and stuck my head outside
so he wouldn't see me start to cry

He got in the car a few minutes later,
wiping the sweat off of his forehead
with his neatly pressed white handkerchief
and patted me on the head and said,
"Don't worry, I'll get you a new one tomorrow."
I tried to smile but I couldn't.
I just sat there thinking of my bike all bent
up and broken hoping there wouldn't be
any traffic on the way to his house
The next day we got up early
and went to this big department store
on Grand Avenue in Maspeth, Queens
where my grandmother lived
and as soon as we walked in the front door
he grabbed the manager by the arm
and asked him where the bicycles were.
"Aisle six," the manager said,
as he pulled his arm away and
looked at me, shaking his head

I started to get nervous when I saw
all the new bikes lined up in a row.
some had banana seats and some
had regular seats, some had thick
tires that were good for riding on rocks and
grass and some had really shiny metal frames
that seemed to glow under the bright lights
of the store but they all were too big
to fit in the trunk of his car

He seemed like he was in a better mood
and I didn't want to spoil it so I started
looking around for something else
that he could buy me, something that
would fit in his car and wouldn't
make him mad at me. that's when I asked
him if he could get me a skateboard

instead of a bicycle. he asked me if I was sure
that's what I wanted and I said yes
some of the guys had them and I
always wanted one, which wasn't true at all

When we got back to his car
I laid the skateboard carefully
on the back seat with the wheels up
so it wouldn't move, then joined him
in the front seat as we drove to the park

When we got there, he sat on a bench
next to his car and read the newspaper
while I walked to the side of the park
where the concrete tennis courts were.
it was March and the nets weren't up yet
because it was too cold to play tennis so
I had the long row of courts all to myself.

I never used a skateboard before but it looked
pretty easy so I put it down on the concrete,
and tried to step on it with my left foot as I pushed
off with my right foot but I lost my balance
and the skateboard slipped out from under me
and started rolling away. after I ran and got it
I tried again, this time putting my right foot
on the skateboard and pushing off with my left foot
but the same thing happened. after a few more tries
I finally got both feet on the skateboard at the same time
but I started going too fast and fell backward,
hitting my head on the concrete, scraping both elbows
and my right shoulder on the way down.

I just laid there on the ground for a few minutes
looking up at the trees and the squirrels having so
much fun running all around, jumping from branch
to branch talking to each other in squirrel language

10

wondering if anyone had found my bike and fixed it
and was riding around the neighborhood sitting
up high on the banana seat holding the handlebars
weaving in and out of the parked cars having so
much fun when I suddenly jumped up and grabbed
the skateboard and started smashing it on one
of the park benches as hard as I could. I kept
smashing it and smashing it until it finally broke
in half. my hands were red and I was out of breath.
then I picked up both pieces of the skateboard
and threw them against the chain-link fence surrounding
the tennis courts. one of the wheels came flying off
and rolled into the street. I just left it there.
then I sat down on the ground and wiped my nose.
I saw him looking at me through the fence
but he didn't say a word. when I got back to his car
I threw the pieces of the skateboard in the back seat
and sat up front with him.
he asked me if I was hungry and I said yes.
then he patted me on the head
and we drove to the diner and had lunch.

apple juice

New Year's Eve 1968
I sat with my father
watching college football
on tv

at 12:00 we toasted
Happy New Year!
with glasses
of apple juice

I remember thinking
that grown-ups
usually go out on
New Year's Eve

but this year
he stayed with me

Thank You

I remember walking with you to the schoolyard
early in the morning when no one was around
with the bicycle you bought me for my birthday.

I liked the sound of the tires as they rolled through
the leaves and puddles of rain that fell the night before
and when we got to the schoolyard you held
the seat of the bicycle with one hand and the
handlebars with your other hand and I sat down
and put my feet on the pedals and you ran next
to me as I started to pedal but I lost my balance
and almost tipped over but you caught me
and said don't worry that happens to everyone
the first time they try so I sat up straight
and started to pedal again but the handlebars
twisted all around and the front tire almost hit you
but you moved out of the way as I steadied myself
and was able to stay on the bicycle for a few seconds
before my foot slipped and the bicycle skidded
on the ground but you held on to me before I fell
and we kept on going and I tried my best to keep
the handlebars straight but they started turning
one way so I tried to turn them back the other way
but I went too far and the front wheel spun
all the way around and I tipped over then the bicycle
fell on top of me and you fell on top of the bicycle
and I was scared that you got hurt so I squeezed myself
out from under the bicycle and tried to pick you up
but I couldn't and we both started laughing
when I fell down next to you and you said maybe
this wasn't such a good idea then smiled and said
you were only kidding then you asked me if I was ready
to try again and I said yes and we both stood up
and you picked up the bicycle and kissed a little bruise

that I got on my elbow and I was about to try again
when these two older boys came into the schoolyard
and I thought they were going to make fun of me
but they didn't they asked if we needed some help
and you said "just a little" and smiled then
one of the boys grabbed one side of the bicycle
and the other boy grabbed the other side of the bicycle and
I got on and started pedaling trying to keep my balance and
the two boys were running next to me holding me up
telling me to keep going and I was steering the bicycle as
straight as I could when it started to shake a little but I kept
holding on to the handlebars feeling the air on my face
watching the schoolyard passing me by, the swings,
the monkey bars, the basketball court, and I didn't realize
that the two boys had let go of the bicycle I just kept on
pedaling until I heard you scream, "you did it! you did
it!" and I looked down at my feet and both of them were
still on the pedals then I looked up at you waving at me
and I just kept on going around the schoolyard and I
was so happy that I forgot to say thank you

And Now We Are Going to South America

After school we would play in the schoolyard
punchball or stickball or tag and when we got tired of tag
we would roll up pieces of looseleaf paper we ripped
out of our notebooks and squeeze them together as tight
as we could then wrap rubber bands around them
until we had a ball of paper big enough to play
our own version of volleyball which went like this:
we made two teams one on each side of this big gray
pipe that ran across one of the entranceways to the
schoolyard and it was just a foot or so above our heads
and all you had to do was get the ball over the pipe
that was it and you got one point if you got it over by
catching it and throwing it over two points if you got it
over by punching or slapping it over and three points if you
got it over by hitting it with a stick or anything like a stick
that you found on the ground or brought with you to school
or took from class like one of those long three-foot rulers
that every math and science teacher had and we just kept
going back and forth adding up the points and after about
an hour or so or until we lost count of the score we would
stop and go home just to put our books down, change our
clothes, and get something to eat, some cookies, a
doughnut, a bag of potato chips, anything we could get our
hands on then we'd meet up again and continue where we
left off or make up some other game that no one ever heard
of except us and we could play it whenever we wanted to
and no one could stop us.

That's the way it was nearly every day after school except
for the day when we found out our part in the class
play. That day I left the game early and ran home to
surprise her because I knew that me being in the class play
would make her happy and lately she hadn't been very
happy.

I opened the front door to our apartment with the key
I kept tied around my neck with a piece of string
and hid next to the refrigerator which I had to push
away from the wall with both hands but even then
the refrigerator only moved a couple of inches
which was just enough for me to squeeze in
as I leaned against the flowered wallpaper
waiting for her to come home from work
which was usually around five o'clock.

I got bored waiting so I started tracing the flowered
pattern of the wallpaper with my fingers going over the
different flowers making believe each finger was a
paintbrush brushing the flowers all different colors red
orange green and blue but mostly blue because blue
was my favorite color and then I started painting over a
leak that ran down the wall from the ceiling painting all
around it in big blue circles until the leak was covered over
and then I started on the opposite wall only this time I
made the circles red because the top of our kitchen table
was red and I wanted them to match.

I kept on doing this until I heard her open the front door
and start walking down the long hallway to the kitchen
with two big bags of groceries in her arms
and I popped out from behind the refrigerator
and told her not to worry that I was ok
and the reason I was here and not with my friends
was that I wanted to surprise her and tell her
that I was in the class play and that the minute I found
out all I could think of was running home and telling her
but she didn't say anything she just looked at me
so I kept on talking telling her how we all had to line up
in the back of the classroom and read different lines
from different scenes in the play and that if she didn't
know what scenes were they were different parts of a play
or movie and how much fun it was to make believe you

were somebody else even for a few minutes and I kept on
waiting for her to say something but she didn't she just
stood there in the middle of the kitchen when suddenly the
two bags of groceries slipped out of her hands and fell to
the floor as she bent down to hug me.

I tried to hug her back but all I could do was hook
my fingers in the loops of her gray winter coat
and I held on as tight as I could as she started to cry
burying her face deep into my shoulder and I told her
I was sorry and that I didn't mean to make her cry
and that I wouldn't be in the play if she didn't want me to
and we both just stayed there on the kitchen floor
for I don't remember how long until she finally let go
and after she brushed the hair away from her face
and wiped her eyes with a tissue she took from
her pocketbook she smiled and kissed me and I felt
so good that I didn't do anything to make her sad
and she asked me what my lines were
and I told her that I didn't have any *real* lines
I only had *words* and there were eight of them:

"And Now We Are Going to South America"

and that I was the first person the audience was going to
see in the play and my teacher said that even though I
didn't have a lot of words to say I had a very important part
because it was the official start of the play and that I had
the loudest voice in the class and that's a very good
talent to have and that's why she picked me for the part.

She immediately started repeating the words: "And Now
We Are Going to South America, And Now We Are Going
to South America" over and over and over again as we
started to pick up the groceries from the floor and she said
that we had to practice my line every day if I was going to
get it right but I said to her that I already knew my line and

she said that didn't matter what mattered was that I was a
"real actor" now and real actors always practiced their lines
so for the next few weeks every time I called her on the
phone
or she came home from work
or put me to bed
or we ate dinner
or we watched tv
or we went to the store
or we washed the dishes
or we folded the laundry
or we played in the park
or we rode on the bus
or we said good morning
or we said goodnight
or whenever else she got the chance
she would make me say:

"And Now We Are Going to South America"

We were the first ones at school the day of the play
and she was talking to some of the other mothers
behind the stage telling them how proud she was
of me and how hard I practiced
and even though I only had eight words to say
it was ok because she was happy
and no matter how hard I tried
I couldn't remember her smiling so much
then a few minutes before the play started
she came over to me and told me
that she had a surprise for me
but that she left it by her seat
and I tried to think of what it could be
and the more I thought about it
the more excited I got so after a while I just gave up and
ran as fast as I could past the other kids and their mothers
practicing their lines

past the costume racks filled with costumes
past the color guard holding all the flags
past the kids in the band who were practicing the Star-
Spangled Banner and other songs from the play
because I loved surprises so much
and I couldn't wait to see what she got me
and the second I pulled opened the curtains
I knew what it was and it was way better
then anything else I could think of.

I saw his green sanitation pants and pressed beige
sanitation shirt as he stepped out from behind one of the
columns of the auditorium and I knew that he saw me too
because he lifted up his arms and I started to run to him
like I always did whenever I saw him forgetting where I
was or what I was doing and the next thing I knew I was
jumping off of the stage and into his arms and he held me
up high above his head, so high that I could see the
paintings on the ceiling of the auditorium and the lights and
the balcony starting to fill up with people and I felt his
strong hands wrapped around me and when he brought me
down to where I could touch his face I remembered just
how much I missed him.

They sat together in the front row and when I came out on
stage I was a little nervous because there were so many
people in the auditorium but then I saw them sitting there
looking at me and they were together and they were happy
and even though I knew that he had to leave sometime after
the play was over that was ok because he was here now and
she was here now and they were here together and they
were smiling and suddenly I wasn't nervous anymore and I
walked to the front of the stage and everyone got really
quiet because they knew that the play was about to start
and I looked at everyone looking at me quiet and waiting
and in as loud a voice as I could I shouted:

"And Now We Are Going to South America!"

and everyone in the audience started to clap, even the kids
that were about to go on stage clapped and my teacher
came over to me as I ran back behind the curtain and said,
"Well I guess I picked the right person to start things off,"
then I stood next to the other kids who were not on stage
yet and every few minutes I would stick my head out
from behind the curtain to make sure they were still sitting
there.

After the play was over and we all took our bows, I ran
down the steps of the stage and took them by the hand and
introduced them to all of my friends' parents proud that
they were here and that they were together and I even went
up to my principal and said, "Here are my parents" and she
smiled and told me what a great job I did then I ran back on
stage one more time and shouted:

"And Now We Are Going to South America"

and everyone who was still in the auditorium started to clap
and I was so happy that I started to clap too.

It was so quiet in the car as he drove us home that I could
hear the click of my mother's pocketbook as she took out
her makeup and patted her cheeks in the side-view mirror
while he kept both of his hands tightly squeezed on the
steering wheel and I was just sitting in the back seat hoping
that maybe this time he would stay a little longer because
back then while most kids my age were dreaming about
being Mickey Mantle I was dreaming about having dinner
with both of my parents, even if it was after the school
play, but as he pulled up to our apartment building he said
that he was sorry but he had to get back to work and after
he said goodbye to both of us we just stood there watching

him drive down the street hoping that maybe he would surprise us and come back around the corner but he never did.

I thought about changing my clothes and going outside to play with my friends but I really didn't feel like it so I just went into the living room and started watching tv but there was nothing on I liked so I went and got my bookbag and took out some comic books to read and the volleyball that we played with yesterday was there so I took it with me into the living room and I sat on the floor by the couch and started throwing it up in the air and catching it first with my right hand, then with my left hand, then with both hands, then I threw it against the wall behind me, flipping it backwards over my head to see if I could catch it without looking when it came back down. That was ok for a while then I started thinking about the play and being in the auditorium with all of my friends and their parents and all of the noise that was going on around me the band playing and people clapping and waving to their kids on stage but then all of a sudden everything in the auditorium started to disappear and the faces of the people were all fuzzy and hard to see and I was looking for them but they weren't there and I started to get upset after a few seconds because I couldn't find them and then I couldn't remember anything about the play even though it was just a few hours ago and that made me sad and then I started to think of him and how I had to wait a whole week before I saw him again and how none of my friends had to wait a whole week to see their fathers and then I started thinking about how I only had eight words to say in the play and that I didn't have any *real* lines because I didn't *really* talk to anyone else in the play I just yelled *really* loud at the audience and that wasn't *really* acting and the more I thought about it the more I started to hate today and I wished that it never happened, none of it, not being on stage, not him coming to surprise me, not seeing them smile, not riding in the car with them, not anything and I promised myself that if my teacher asked me to be in the play next year, I would tell her that I wouldn't do it no matter how much she liked the sound of my voice.

She came into the living room a few minutes later and asked me what I was doing. I told her nothing I was just playing with this stupid ball that we played this stupid made-up volleyball game with after school and then she asked me if she could see the "stupid" ball so I kicked it over to her and she started to laugh when she picked it up and saw that it was made of looseleaf paper and rubber bands and I asked her why she was laughing and then she sat down next to me on the floor and said that when she was a little girl my grandparents didn't have a lot of money so my uncle and her used fill up brown paper bags with air by crinkling the top edges of each bag together but leaving a little open space and blowing into it until the bag filled up with air like a paper balloon then whoever wasn't holding the bag would run and get some string and tie the edges together really tight so that none of the air would come out and then they would break off the extra string and have a catch or kick the blown up bag around my grandparents' apartment and the best thing about their paper ball was that it was so light it couldn't knock any furniture or lamps over or break any windows and I thought wow what a great idea and when she said do you want me to show you how we used to make one I said sure but she said first I had to explain the volleyball game to her and I did and she said that doesn't seem like a *stupid* game and I said well I guess it really isn't then she got up and went into the kitchen and came back with a couple of brown paper bags and some string and a pair of scissors and then she showed me how to crinkle up the edges of the bag and make the space to blow into it and I started to blow up one of the bags and I couldn't believe it but it really did blow up like a brown paper balloon and when it was almost full she said hold the edges together really tight and then she cut a piece of string with the scissors and tied the edges together and when she was done I threw it up in the air and watched it float around the living room and then we started hitting the brown paper ball to each other and it would bounce off the walls and the couch and the chair by the window and when it would hit the floor we just scooped it up and started hitting it again and it really was a lot of fun then she said wait a minute I have an idea and she took the ball of string and tied one end of the string to this old metal light that was attached to one of the walls then she walked to the opposite wall and took down the picture that was hanging there and tied the other end of the string around the hook that held the picture up and I figured out what she was doing then I gave her the scissors and she cut the rest of the string off and the string was just high enough above my head for me to reach it on my tip-toes which wasn't as high as the big gray pipe in the schoolyard but that was ok we were inside anyway and then I stood on one side of the string and she stood on the other side of the string and I explained the rules of our volleyball game to her one more time just so she wouldn't forget them and then we started playing throwing the ball over the string smacking it off of the walls and ceiling jumping up and hitting it with our hands (she even tried to kick it over one time which none of us ever did) then she took her slipper off and hit the ball so hard it ripped right down the middle and all of the air came out and it almost landed on my head as it floated to the floor and we both started laughing so hard we couldn't speak and just like that the world was ok again.

banana sandwich

you lifted me up
above the refrigerator
where the bananas were

I picked one
and gave it to you
then you flattened it out
between two pieces of bread

such a delicious sandwich

Anytime She Wants To

The first car I ever bought was a used 1974 Plymouth Duster. It had about 47,000 miles on it. Not bad for a five-year-old car I thought. It turns out that I was wrong. More than likely that Duster had 147,000 miles on it, because it only lasted a year and a half, from May 1979 to October 1980. I was in graduate school at the University of Connecticut for Adaptive Physical Education when the engine seized on Christmas Eve. Luckily, I was home in Brooklyn at the time, and my friend Scott lent me his car until I completed my master's degree in July of 1981. I found a teaching job a few weeks later, but it was in Douglaston, Queens, which meant I needed a car to get there. This one, I promised myself, was going to be brand new.

I started saving coins in this big glass water cooler jug when I was around ten or eleven years old. At first, I put any coin I could find in the jug, but when I was around fifteen, I started to only put quarters in it. Why have all those smaller coins take up valuable space? I thought. My mother had to move the year I went away to Connecticut, and she told me that my jug of coins was so heavy it took three movers to pick it up and load it onto the moving van.

One of my friends took me around to about four or five different car dealerships, and I finally decided to buy a no-frills, two-door Toyota Corolla. I was only twenty-two years old, and I wasn't very experienced (actually, I wasn't experienced at all) in dealing with car salesmen, so after a few minutes of "negotiating" (which was basically me nodding my head yes to everything he said), we agreed on a price of $4,600. With that settled, the next step was getting the money to pay for the car. That's where the jug full of coins comes in. For the next few days, I poured out all of the coins from the jug on my living room floor, divided them up into pennies, nickels, dimes, and quarters (along with a few half-dollars and silver dollars), and then began the tedious task of stuffing them into these brown paper wrappers that looked like little cylinders until my fingers couldn't take it anymore (back in 1981, we didn't have the luxury of just taking a jar full of coins to the bank and pouring them down a machine and getting cash for it). When I was done, I had approximately $4,300, and even though I was short about $300, my mother said she would make up the difference, along with buying me my first tank of gas. The only thing left to do now was to bring the rolls of coins to the bank and cash them in for actual dollars, which I happily did in about seven or eight exhausting trips.

A few days later my mother and I went to the Toyota Dealership, which was on 4th Avenue and 65th Street, to buy my new car. As soon as I walked through the front door, I went right over to the same salesman I met with the week before. I had a big smile on my face. "I did it," I told him. "I got the $4,600 to buy the Corolla." He slowly lifted his head up from his desk and looked at me. He wasn't smiling. "You are right," he finally said, as he handed me a piece of paper with numbers on it that I couldn't understand. "When we met last week, I did in fact say the Corolla you picked out was $4,600, but that didn't include the registration fee, the inspection fee, the delivery fee, and the license plate fee. When you add all those up, the total comes to $5,100." "Wait a second," I said, as I leaned over his desk. I was pissed. "You told me last week that the car was $4,600. Now you're saying it's $5,100. You're a liar. Just because I'm twenty-two years old you think you can trick me into paying more money than I should. Well, that's not going to happen."

I could feel my face turning red and my hands starting to shake. Suddenly I felt someone tap me on the shoulder. I turned around. It was my mother. I had totally forgotten she was there. She gently pulled me to the side. "Why don't you go outside for a few minutes and let me handle this," she whispered. Then she smiled at me like she knew something I didn't know, so I reluctantly left the dealership and started to walk down 4th Avenue. I was really mad. Did he think I was stupid or something? I wasn't paying $5,100 for a $4,600 car. It didn't even have an air conditioner in it. Suddenly I heard my mother calling me to come back inside. The salesman was standing by the copy machine, copying a packet of papers. He stapled them together, then handed one of the packets to me. I immediately looked down at the price. It said $4,400. Total. I couldn't believe it.

The salesman said he was sorry for any misunderstanding. I said no problem. Then he said he'd be right back. He had to get the manager to sign his copy of the packet. I just looked at my mother. "How the heck did you do that? The price is $200 *less* than what he said it was last week." My mother just winked at me and lifted her skirt halfway up her thigh. "They fall for it *all* the time," she said. I may be forty-eight years old, but I still got it. And I can use it anytime I want to."

Little Boots

My father's nickname was Boots. When he was around ten years old, he started shoveling all of the houses in his neighborhood during the winter when it snowed. He charged twenty-five cents for each house and fifty cents for each apartment building. He would get up early in the morning when it was still dark outside, and shovel all day long until late at night. He told me one time he made over twenty-five dollars shoveling snow, which was a lot of money in 1933. One day it snowed nearly ten inches, and my grandmother told my father not to go outside because the snow was too deep and he might get hurt. My father didn't listen to her, and when he went down to the basement of his building to get a shovel, he found a pair of old black boots in the garbage. He put them on and went outside to start shoveling, and from then on, he was known as Boots to everyone in the neighborhood. My uncle Frank even used the name Boots when he wrote my father's obituary in 1978.

My mother was three months pregnant when she went to her gynecologist for a routine exam. There were about three or four other women in the waiting room, and they were all having babies too. One of the women asked my mother how many months pregnant she was. When my mother said three months, the woman was surprised because my mother's stomach wasn't very big. In fact, if she didn't say anything, none of the women in the waiting room would have known that my mother was even pregnant. After the exam was over, the doctor told my mother that he didn't hear a heartbeat and there didn't seem to be any movement from the fetus. He suggested that my mother take a pill to dispose of the fetus, because there was a good chance that it wasn't alive, and he didn't want my mother to be in any danger because of that. My mother had always known that something wasn't right since she had gotten pregnant, but she never imagined that she might be carrying a dead baby inside of her. She was so upset that she had to call my father at work to pick her up and take her home. The next day my mother took a bus to my grandmother's house and told her what the doctor said to do. My grandmother was a strong, gray-haired, Hungarian woman who had lost two children of her own when she was around my mother's age, and she knew the pain that my mother was going through. She told my mother that she shouldn't listen to the doctor, and that she should wait and give birth to the baby, even if it wasn't alive, because that was the right thing to do. And so once a month, my mother would go to her gynecologist's office and sit in the waiting room with all of the other mothers whose stomachs were growing round and full with life, while all she had was a tiny bump that barely showed through her dress. And while the other mothers were waiting for the doctor to see them, they would knit all sorts of beautiful things for their babies. One mother knitted a few sweaters in different colors, another mother knitted a big checkered blanket to wrap around her baby when it was born, and one of the mothers even knitted matching hats for her and her twin baby boys. And just so the other mothers wouldn't ask her any questions, my mother started knitting a pair of boots, even though she knew that her baby would probably never wear them. Then one night, around five months later, my mother told my father that she was in labor, and that it was time to take her to the hospital. My parents weren't excited because they already knew what to expect, and were silent for the entire car ride there. When they got to the hospital the doctor was waiting for them. He took my mother into an operating room while my father waited outside in the hallway. After a few hours the doctor said that my mother was about to give birth, and he reminded her that it would probably not be a fully formed baby. But when the doctor reached inside of my mother, he felt the umbilical cord wrapped three times around the baby's neck, and when he cut it, the baby let out a long, deep breath, and started to wiggle around in the doctor's hands. My mother couldn't speak when the doctor handed the baby to her and told her that it was a boy. She didn't believe any of it was real. All she could do was hold the baby close to her and tell him how much she loved him and how much she would always love him. When my father came into the room a few minutes later, he just stood at the door watching my mother holding me. He was too nervous to go inside. When my mother saw him, she told him to come over and see his son. He sat down next to her on the bed and started to cry. Then she took his hand and put it on my stomach. He pulled it away. "Don't worry," she said, as she gently put his hand back on my stomach. "He's fine. Really, he's fine. Aren't you, little Boots? You're fine. You're really, really fine."

Go Figure

I saw him punch a wall
I saw him break a chair
I saw him smash a glass vase
I saw him throw a radio through a window
I saw him bang a metal garbage can on the roof of his car
I saw him stomp on a toy that didn't work
I saw him crack a baseball bat in half
I saw him kick in a car door when he locked his keys inside
I saw him rip out a desk drawer when he couldn't open it
I saw him pull a closet door off its hinges
I saw him mangle a bicycle when it wouldn't fit in his car
I saw him throw a bowling ball over a fence
I saw him push a piece of furniture down a flight of stairs
I saw him dump a bag of groceries on the kitchen floor
I saw him beat the hood of his car when he got a flat tire
I saw him tear a shirt to pieces when a button fell off
I saw him destroy a folding table when it wouldn't stand
I saw him scream at my mother until she cried

I also saw him get out of his car in the middle
of traffic to help a blind man cross the street

Friendship

Friendship plain and simple is smooth with
no visible edges, symmetrically clear in its natural
beauty like a ball made of glass dangling in front of you
slowly dropping into your hand, the curve of your palm
supporting it while your fingers gently surround it;
to the naked eye it seems like you are holding it,
when in reality, it is holding you

Do Over

Hours after he dropped me off
I walked to the corner where everyone
was hanging out and we chose up a game
of punchball four or five of us on a side
but first we cleared away any garbage
that was on the sidewalk
then flipped for who'd hit first

Phil lost and we took the field
I walked to the mailbox we used
as first base, thinking of him
and wondering if he got home ok

Eddie flied out and Chris smacked a double
past the awning of the new apartment building
they just built across the street then Jack
hit a home run a huge shot off the wall of the
firehouse that only three of us had ever done before
but I didn't care much because I was trying
to figure out where he was and if he'd be home
when I called him later on tonight

Tommy hit a liner that popped off of Freddie's
hand but John dove and made a really great catch,
then Sal hit a long shot over a row of double-parked
cars but Joey, with those long arms of his,
grabbed it before it hit the windshield
of this brand-new Buick, saving a sure double

I usually lead off but didn't feel much like hitting
so they put me last which was ok for today
in fact I thought about going home as soon as I got there
but what good would that do I already cried enough
for two days and I didn't want my mother to worry

any more than she usually did when he took me home

There were two outs when Freddie singled
and John hit the top of the fence that
surrounded the empty lot we played football
in when it snowed and we were ahead
by three runs when Joey gave me the ball,
a brand-new Spalding "High Bounce Ball,"
the letters starting to fade after a day of smacks
and dives and scrapes and long throws from the outfield
and said, "Finish them off"

I started to turn the ball over in my hands
to get a good feel for it as I looked
over the field when suddenly everything
around me started to smell like him and then
I remembered that just a couple of hours ago I was
hugging him like I always did when we said
goodbye and would come away smelling like him
which lasted for a few minutes but was enough
for me to see his face, his smile, his high cheekbones
and I could feel my eyes start to swell up
but I didn't want anyone to see me like this
so I bent down pretending to tie my shoelaces
when Chris called out, "Let's go already!"
and I slowly walked over to the cardboard square
that we used as home plate

I put him out of my mind as best as I could
but quickly lost sight of the ball when I tossed it up
in the air, missing it completely, the embarrassment
of that freezing me in my tracks

I let the ball bounce in front of me, watching it
roll off the curb still standing there frozen
like a statue as Tommy and Jack ran in from
across the street laughing and patting each other

on the back when suddenly Sal called out, "Do over!"
and everyone just stopped where they were
and looked at him, "I was fixing my sleeve," he said,
as the muscles in his neck started to bulge
which scared everyone back to where they were
and he just looked at me as if he knew and I
wiped my face and picked up the ball from the gutter
and smacked a double off a passing milk truck
my hair blowing in my face as I rounded second base

Plastic Bags and Tube Socks

Gus was a year or two older than us and he was about
fifteen at the time when he told us one day while we were
in the middle of a stickball game that the night before he
had sex with Lori Rubin and that it wasn't the first time
that he had sex with a girl so we immediately stopped
playing and bought ice cream sandwiches from the Good
Humor man who was on the corner watching us play and
sat down to listen to what happened to Gus the night before
and it was really so interesting that Chris didn't take one
bite of his ice cream sandwich and Gus had to stop talking
for a minute or so because the ice cream sandwich had
melted all the way down Chris's left hand and arm and
when he finally cleaned it up and bought another one
which he remembered to eat this time Gus continued on
with his story and when he got up to the part when he put
his penis in Lori's vagina which Gus said was the part of
sex that was called intercourse all of us stopped moving
around and just sat there pretty still and quiet pulling at our
napkins and wondering how that must feel and when Gus
was done with his story Phil asked him and Gus said that if
we really wanted to know how it felt all we had to do was
go home and fill up a small plastic bag with warm water
and put our penises in it which the thought of doing
something like that made us all laugh but I have to admit
that later on when Gus was finished answering all of our
other questions I ran home and made sure my mother
wasn't around and locked myself in the bathroom and did
what Gus said and stood there for I think it was almost half
an hour but nothing really happened except that my penis
felt a little cold after a while and then got real small and
blue which made me a little scared but after that nothing
really to speak of except that when I took my penis back
out of the plastic bag all of the water spilled down my left
leg and pretty much soaked my tube sock so I took it off

36

and had dinner as if nothing happened then went outside
and met everyone and that's when Gus started laughing
and said that he was joking about the plastic bag and warm
water being like a vagina and we all started laughing too
only when we sat down pretty much all of us had only one
tube sock on

Birthday Present

It was snowing when I got out of the train station
big white chunks coming down in bunches
all over my head and in my face
the snow melting down my cheeks and neck
all the way down my back it felt cold but good
after the long train ride and the long day of classes.

I stood at the top of the steps to the station
watching the snow fall on the streetlights and the passing
cars and the canopies of the office buildings that lined the
sidewalk and the people walking home from work
with their scarves blowing in the wind
and their hats rolling on the ground
holding their briefcases and shopping bags over their
heads and I watched them run past me down the steps
to the station slipping and sliding and tripping
as millions of snowflakes followed behind them.

I stuck out my hand as I started to walk along the streets
and caught a few flakes of snow that were falling down
they melted fast and soon more flakes fell in their place
and they melted just as fast until my hand was filled with
water that tasted fresh and cold and good and I took a few
sips until it was all gone and while the streets filled up with
snow and the hum of traffic went by I stuck my books
under my coat buttoned it up as far as it would go then put
my hands in my pockets and walked to the corner my
tracks disappearing behind me along with the people and
the buildings and the cars and the canopies and everything
else that was around.

I got to the restaurant before she did and walked inside
it was empty and the waiters were setting up the tables for
dinner when one of them saw me and asked if I wanted a

table and I told him that I was waiting for someone and he smiled and said that I could choose any table I wanted and I thanked him and told him that I would be back soon then I pushed open the door and was back out in the clean fresh snow-filled night again.

Outside of the restaurant the streets were white and empty and the lights from the stores across the street were off and the stores were black inside except for one near the corner, an old Army and Navy store and I crossed the street and went over to the window where the lights were still on and all the jackets and hats and winter clothes that they sold hung from thick wooden hooks and I looked at all of them hanging there and they all looked so warm and new and strong and I brushed away some of the snow that stuck to the window of the store and in the back row there was a brown leather Air Force bomber jacket with brown fur around the collar and yellow fur inside and a thick silver zipper down the front and it stood out among all of the other jackets and I just looked at it hanging there wishing I could climb inside that window and take it out when no one was looking and put it on and I even put my hands on the glass of the window to get as close as I could to it.

I pictured myself taking the jacket off of the wooden hook and putting it on and walking through the streets with the collar up and the snow falling on it and sliding off down the back and people looking at me wearing that jacket with my hands in the fur-lined pockets and me feeling proud and strong and fearless just walking along while everyone looked at me jealous of who I was and what I was wearing and the fact that nothing could ever hurt me again no matter what as long as I wore that jacket. I didn't see her walk across the street but I knew it was her when she put her hand on my shoulder and stood next to me looking in the window and said: "It really is a beautiful jacket," and

39

I wondered how she knew I was looking at that exact
one with all of the other jackets in the window but she
always "knew" things like that and then she said something
else but I didn't hear her I was still caught up in the dream
of wearing that jacket and walking down the street with all
the people looking at me and then I blurted out: "I bet
nothing could touch me in that jacket" and she smiled and
said: "I bet you're right" then a man inside the store tapped
on the window and motioned for us to come inside.

I guess there wasn't anything else for him to do on a night
like this and when we didn't come in the man came out to
us he opened the door and his tie blew back across his face
from the wind and some snow blew in the store and he
tried to kick it away but even he started laughing at that
then he asked me if I liked the jacket and I said who
wouldn't like a jacket like that and he said that it was on
sale for only eighty dollars and I just smiled and said
thanks but we had to go to dinner and he asked me if I
wanted to try it on and I said no but she said sure why not
and I just looked at her and said it's ok let's just go eat
because I knew that if I put it on I would never want to take
it off and I couldn't do that to myself or to her because
once she saw me put the jacket on and saw the way it made
me feel she would want to buy it for me but she really
couldn't afford it and I didn't want her to feel worse than
she already did about things so I thanked him again and
looked at the jacket one last time then we left the store the
wind blowing the door shut behind us.

We didn't say anything as we walked across the street to
the restaurant waiting first by the curb while a line of
sanitation trucks passed by with their heavy metal shovels
scraping the ground and the chains from their big black
tires whirling around clicking and clacking as they made
little canals of snow which we followed until we got to the
other side of the street and went inside the restaurant where

the same waiter I met a few minutes ago greeted us with the same smile that he had on for me and said that he saved a table just for us which made me laugh because the restaurant was still empty.

After we sat down, we looked at the menus the waiter handed us and drank some water which the busboy set down along with a setting each of a napkin, fork, soup spoon, and knife and a basket of bread that was burned around the edges which meant that it was a day old and they wanted to make it seem like they were warming it up just for us which was ok because the butter melted faster when the bread was hot and we were both very hungry.

Her face was still red from the cold a few minutes later when she asked me if I needed her to type my final paper and I told her that I would handwrite it and she said that I should really type it because I wasn't in high school anymore, and that I had better get used to doing more "college-aged things" like doing my own laundry and ironing my own shirts and opening a checking account so I could start writing checks to build up my credit score (whatever that meant) and while she kept listing all of the things that I needed to do, all I could think about was that leather Air Force bomber jacket hanging in the window of the Army and Navy store across the street and when I would wear it and all of the places I would wear it to and how good I would look wearing it and what I would wear under it sometimes a sweatshirt, sometimes just a t-shirt, sometimes a heavy sweater on days like this when it was cold and snowing and how all the guys would want to try it on when they saw me wearing it and how I wouldn't let them and how jealous they would get when we would go places together and everyone there would be looking at me wearing my jacket and I would smile to myself knowing that this jacket was *my* jacket and no one else's jacket and when I looked up I saw the way my mother was looking at me (because she knew what I was thinking) and I knew what was coming next so I just handed her my napkin and told her she was going to need it which made her laugh instead of the other thing which always made me sad and a little while later after we were done eating she asked for the check and I told her I had to go to the bathroom and she said that was fine because she needed some air and she'd be waiting for me outside which was her way of saying that she was going to smoke a cigarette but when I was done and went outside I didn't see her anywhere until I walked across the street and there she was inside the Army and Navy store talking to that same man and I watched them talking, not being able to move, my breath forming little white breath clouds that landed on the front window of the store and when I rubbed them off I saw her shaking her head and closing her pocketbook then turning around like she was going to leave but the man stopped her and after a few minutes of hand waving and head nodding she opened her pocketbook again and that's when I knew so I pushed open the door and ran over to her and before I could say anything she started pulling off my coat, the one my cousin gave me a few years ago when it got too small for him to wear then I heard the man come up behind me and I turned around and he gave me the jacket *my* jacket and I carefully put it on sliding my right arm in first then my left arm and I lifted up the collar and put my hands in the pockets which made a crinkling sound and she said, "aren't you going to zip it up?" but I didn't hear her by then I was standing in front of a mirror in the middle of the store looking at the jacket in the window that was now on me and it was mine it was really mine and it fit just right and I felt strong and brave and I saw her looking at me but I couldn't think of anything to say so I just looked at myself in the mirror, happier than I had been in a long long time.

It was crowded on the train going home people moving and
pushing and running for seats people in suits and dresses
and jackets made of wool and overcoats and gloves and
hats falling to the floor bending down to pick them up
bumping into other people who either made faces or
bumped them back and with each stop it got more and
more crowded as I leaned against the door of the train
feeling the pushing and shoving and bouncing back and
forth as the fur of my jacket brushed up against my face so
warm and soft and I held up my arm to grab one of the
handles of the train and looked at it covered in leather and
heard the clink of the metal zipper as the train came to a
sudden stop and my body moved forward just a bit,
bumping the man in front of me who quickly turned around
to see who it was that bumped him then quickly turned
back around as I thought, "Yeah, that's right, it was ME."

When we finally got off at our stop and walked up the
stairs to the street we saw all the Christmas decorations in
the trees and on the front lawns of some of the houses on
our block and there were lights blinking on and off in some
of the windows yellow and white with candles and stars
and letters spelling out HAPPY HOLIDAYS and when we
came to our apartment building I said that I would be up in
a few minutes and she kissed me on the forehead as I
wrapped my arms around her letting her know just how
much all of this meant to me.

I started walking up and down the street
making little mountains of snow with my boots
then squashing them like I did when I was a kid
and I raised my arms up high above my head
like Sylvester Stallone did in "Rocky"
after he ran up the stairs in Philadelphia,
shadow-boxing my reflection in a car window
"boom-boom" "bam-bam" "boom-boom-boom"
weaving in and out of a row of trees

dancing on my tip-toes
throwing jabs and uppercuts and left-hooks
until I got to the corner
and I just stood there, listening to the night
still and quiet and empty
except for the sound of a window closing
just above my head.

windshield wipers

I watched you drive
down the block after
you dropped me off

the rain had just started
and I wondered if
you turned on the
windshield wipers

last time
you forgot

Guilty

One night we were all hanging out when this girl from school came walking by. Nobody was really friends with her, we just knew her from school and all the rumors that were going around about her. She would have sex with you for five dollars, or give you a blowjob for one dollar. She said she didn't give handjobs because she didn't want to get her hands dirty which we all thought made no sense at all. Everyone at school would make fun of her when they saw her. I felt bad because her parents were divorced like mine, but I didn't talk to her or anything because I didn't want everyone to start making fun of me too. When she saw us, she came right over. One of my friends started to smile. "What's up?" he said. "Nothing much," she said. "I'm just bored." We all knew what that meant. My friend put his hand in his pocket and took out a dollar and gave it to her. She followed him around the corner and down an alley that was between two apartment buildings in the middle of the block. A few minutes later they came back. My friend was smiling, holding his crotch, while the girl just walked over to the rest of us like nothing happened. Then all of a sudden, my friend put his hand on my shoulder and said to the girl, "You know, he's never had a blowjob before." "Really?" she said. "Yeah, really." Then he threw a dollar at her. "Here's your next customer." He caught me by surprise. "I'm not doing this," I said, when I realized what was going on. "Don't be a pussy," my friend said. "I'm not being a pussy. You're the one who's being a pussy." I was starting to get pissed. "You can't even get a regular girl to give you a blowjob. You have to get her." The words just shot out of my mouth. I looked at the girl who picked up the dollar. "I didn't mean it like that." She just shook her head. "Are you coming or not?" I didn't want to do this. Not here. Not with her. She was disgusting, my friend was disgusting, this whole thing was disgusting.

"That's ok, I'm good," I said. "Let someone else go." My friend threw another dollar at the girl. "Make sure you do a good job." Everyone started laughing. I didn't know what to do. My friend was right. I never had a blowjob before, and I really wanted one. What's the big deal? I thought. Nobody's going to know about this anyway. It'll only take a few minutes, then it'll be over. So I said yes and followed her around the corner and into the alley. It was dirty as hell, and it smelled like crap. She sat on a wooden milk crate and told me to stand in front of her. I started to shake a little. I couldn't tell if I was excited or afraid someone would see us. "You want me to unbuckle your pants or are you going to do it?" "I'll do it," I said, but the zipper kept getting stuck. "Relax. I'll just do it." Before I knew it my pants were on the ground and I watched her lean over and put my penis in her mouth. I tried to enjoy it, but I kept looking around at the dirty red bricks of the apartment buildings on either side of us, and the broken bottles and milk crates lying in puddles, and bags of garbage ripped open by mice or rats or whatever else lives here, and pieces of food scattered all around. It was horrible, with the smell and water dripping down from leaking pipes and people screaming from open windows and I thought I can't do this, not here, not with her, so I started to pull my penis out of her mouth but it felt warm and good but my mind just kept going on and on about being here with her and not doing this with someone that I liked and I thought I really do sound like a pussy when all of a sudden I heard her say, "Ok, you can pull your pants up now." What? That's it. We're done. I can't believe it. She stood up from the milk crate and wiped her mouth on her coat sleeve. I looked down at my pants, lying on the ground like some dead animal. I felt like shit. I started to say something. "Don't bother," she said, as she started to walk back out of the alley, leaving me all by myself.

47

Little Meatballs

He would usually take me on weekends from Friday afternoon after school let out until Sunday morning and sometimes during the week for dinner if he could get off from work and he would take me every other Thanksgiving and Easter Sunday and a whole week in August when he worked nights at the station and we would spend all day together in the park, playing baseball and hide and seek in the tall grass on the far side of the park that they never remembered to cut and get bologna and mustard sandwiches and orange soda for lunch, and if it was hot enough I would run under the sprinklers with just my shorts on and no t-shirt and he would sit under one of the trees watching me and smiling and he would hug me when I came out and ran over to him, his white shirt starched and pressed, with creases down the sleeves getting soaked with water but he didn't mind I could tell because it was usually me who let go first to go back under the sprinklers, splashing and sliding and tripping on the slippery wet concrete.

Once in a while I would get to spend Christmas Eve with him. That was the best time of all. He would pick me up early in the morning and we would drive to my aunt's house and I would play hide and seek and tag with my cousins running all around, upstairs and downstairs and even in the basement until someone told us to stop which we did until they forgot about us and we started again while my uncle set up the Christmas lights on the windows outside of their house and down the long metal railing which led to the street and even on the fire hydrant in front of his neighbor's house which he made into a little snowman with bright blue eyes and blue hands that moved up and down with a little motor he attached to the back and covered up with a piece of white cloth to make it look like

snow and around the garage door with the big red and
white Santa Claus that switched on and off in different
colors that you could see all the way down their block
when you came around the corner after having Christmas
Eve dinner and went for a walk to make room for dessert
and the sky was black and the stars were sparkling yellow
and sometimes orange-red so big and bright you could
almost touch them.

I would start packing days before he took me, and
sometimes I would pack a whole week's worth of clothes,
shoving shorts and socks and sweaters into my old green
duffel bag, along with a few pairs of pants, my sneakers, a
fresh clean button-down flannel shirt for Christmas Eve
dinner, my favorite stack of comic books, and a small
Zenith transistor radio the one I would listen to for the
weather to see when it was going to snow because if it
snowed and if it snowed long enough and hard enough and
if the flakes of snow were big enough and if it wasn't
sunny out for the snow to melt
and if the streets grew icy at night from all of the snow
that fell and the cold weather that winter brought
then it would be too dangerous to drive
and he couldn't take me back home
and I could stay with him
at least for another day
or maybe even longer.

It was hard to tell who was happier, me or him
when he picked me up in his 1972 blue four-door
Custom Ford, with the plastic still on the seats
that would crinkle when I sat down
and the black floor mats that spelled out F-O-R-D
with big white letters I used to cover with my feet
to spell out different words like O-R and F-O-R
and I would make a "T" out of the "D" by covering
the curved part of it with my right foot to spell out

F-O-R-T and I was so excited to be with him
that I couldn't speak because so many words
wanted to come out of my mouth at the same time
that I couldn't decide which ones to say
so I just sat there next to him
as we drove on the highway
looking out the window
holding my radio in my hand
hoping for the sky to turn white.

When we finally got to my aunt's house I would run
up the steps and push open the front door and scream
hello to everyone as they were busy getting ready for
dinner, setting the table, lighting the candles, bringing in
the glasses, smoothing out the tablecloth, dusting the
lampshades, vacuuming the rug, screaming at each other
"who took the broom," "we're missing a fork," "I already
did that," "that doesn't go there," "yes it does," "where are
the napkins," "did anyone buy flowers," while my
grandmother yelled at them to get out of the way
as she tried to count the chairs that were brought up
from the basement and everyone tried not to laugh
when she lost count then one of my cousins would finally
just make up a number which made my grandmother
happy but it didn't stop her from counting anyway for the
next few hours.

And this is way it was on Christmas Eve
when I would sneak into the kitchen
where the smell of tomatoes and onions and fresh basil
filled the air and I pulled on my aunt's dress
to let her know I was standing next to her
but she was so busy giving directions to everyone
and basting the ham that was in the oven
that she didn't see me (or so I thought)
so I stood up on my tip-toes
trying to get a look at the top of the stove

50

to see if it was there
the small silver pot, *my* silver pot
filled with what she made just for me
and she would smile when she finally saw me
and kiss me on the cheek and whisper,
"Soon, they'll be ready soon"
while she stirred the big pot of sauce with the brown spoon
that each one of my aunts got as a gift from
my grandmother on their fifteenth birthday
then a few minutes later she would turn around
and in the spoon there would be three or four of them,
little meatballs that she took from my pot
and everyone in the kitchen would turn around
and smile as my aunt gently blew on them
so they wouldn't burn the roof of my mouth
and she would reach for a small red-flowered plate
and carefully roll the little meatballs off of her spoon
and onto the plate then hand me a fork
she just rinsed off in the sink
and I would take the plate with both hands
and carefully walk over to the little coffee table
near the kitchen window with the white candle
and small green Christmas tree on it
and I would sit down and slowly drop each meatball
in my mouth they tasted so sweet and warm and delicious
and in between bites I would wipe any tomato sauce
that got on my face with my shirt sleeve
forgetting that I had a napkin on my lap.

On this Christmas Eve there was no snow
but worse than that there was no *sign* of snow,
and as everyone was sitting down to dinner,
passing around plates of ziti, sauce, meatballs,
sausage, salad, broccoli, and fresh-baked Italian bread
I kept looking out of the living room window
where the streets were still clear and the sky was still blue
and I kept on looking for as long as I could

until someone asked me why I wasn't eating and I didn't
know what to say so I got up and went to the bathroom
locked the door took my transistor radio out of my pocket
pulled up the antenna
turned it on
held it close to my ear
and started listening to the weather report,
which wasn't very good.
there was no snow in the forecast for today
and none for tomorrow, or the day after that
and no matter which station I listened to
all the weathermen said the same thing:
"Sunny and cold, with clear skies, and little wind"
so I shut the radio off and just sat there,
on the floor of the bathroom
hoping with all of my might
that the weathermen were wrong
and it would somehow start to snow.

It was dark outside when I finally came out of the
bathroom and I couldn't believe it when I looked outside
but the tops of the trees across the street were covered in
white, and the roofs of the houses were covered in white
too and white flakes were skimming down from my aunt's
living room window and coming to rest on the outside
ledge then spilling over onto the cement driveway below
and I watched as the white flakes continued to fall in
bunches past the streetlights and the doors of the houses
across the street and I couldn't believe it was snowing, it
was really really snowing then suddenly I felt his hand on
my shoulder "Help me clear off the car," he said, as he
opened the front door, "Before it really starts to come
down."

By the time I got outside, he had cleared off most of the car
except for my side, and he threw me the little plastic snow
brush he kept under his seat, and I brushed off my window

and door and kicked off some snow that had gathered on
the back tires when he said, "Better go get your bag.
Doesn't look like it's going to stop anytime soon and I got
to get you home before it gets any worse."

I tried to think of something to say to him
something to make him change his mind,
"The streets look bad, maybe we should stay…"
but I couldn't, I was so upset at the thought
of having to leave, so I just turned around
and started walking back up the steps
when I saw my little cousin waving at me,
trying to push the little pile of snow
off the window ledge from inside the house
pointing to it, then pointing to me, then pointing
to it again but by then I was already inside getting
my bag and kissing everyone goodbye.

I headed towards the front door passing by the living room
window when I saw him standing by the curb looking
down the block as he scooped up a handful of snow from
the hood of his car and made a snowball and threw it at one
of the trees and smiled when he hit a branch and a bunch of
snow fell to the ground then he got in his car and a few
seconds later a small puff of white powder blew out of the
back exhaust, followed by the rumble of the engine
which quickly settled down to an even hum.

My aunt called me over for one last hug
when suddenly the front door opened
and it was him, brushing off his coat
and knocking his shoes together on the door mat.
"Damn thing wouldn't turn over," he said.
"Can you believe that?
And I just had it tuned up last week."
Then he looked over at me, all bundled up next to my aunt.

"Guess we'll have to stay over tonight. Is that ok with you?"

I didn't say a word to him.
I just took off my hat and gloves and ran over
to the dining room table
which was almost cleared off by now
expect for some empty soda bottles
and broken off pieces of Italian bread
and my plate, filled with little meatballs
and I sat down at the table
with my jacket still on
and started eating them,
two and three at a time
and didn't look up
even when I felt him
sit down next to me.

last night

last night
I heard you crying
in the kitchen

the floor was cold
as I inched
closer to you

hoping
you would stop
before
I got there

Grandma

grandma, do you remember when I would go into the back
room of your apartment while you were in the living room
watching tv? what did you say to my father when I went
back there? what did he say to you?
I know you didn't laugh at me. I know you loved me more
than that. were you worried about me?
was my father worried about me? what did he say?
I was only gone a few minutes, maybe half an hour.
did you smell the candle I lit? could you guess why I lit it?
you never asked me what I was doing back there.
you trusted me, right? I know you did.
I know you loved me.
did my father ever sneak up to the door and listen to what I
was doing? I thought I heard him a few times.

I want to tell you what I was doing back there grandma.
I was looking for God.
I wanted him to help me and make me feel better.
I was sad back then when I was fifteen
and I didn't know what to do about it.
I didn't tell any of my friends because I thought they might
make fun of me. I never spoke to my father about it
because I didn't want to bother him. he had so much on his
mind after he got sick and I didn't want to make him feel
worse.

this is what I did, grandma.
I sat on the wooden floor with my legs crossed and my
back straight and lit a candle like it said to do in this book I
got from the library.
it said that was the way to see God.
it said to sit still and close your eyes and picture what you
think God looks like and if you did that enough times and

really meant it he would come to you and maybe even talk
to you and help you feel better.
I thought if I could see God I would be happy
and then I would be able to make my father happy too.
I was very worried about him. he always looked so sad.

I remember I tried it a few times to see what it was like.
It was pretty cool, sitting there on the floor breathing in and
out and looking at the candle and the different colors of the
flame as it moved all around. in the beginning I couldn't sit
for a long time but then I was able to sit for almost twenty
minutes. one time the flame started floating in the air. I
couldn't stop looking at it. it floated right above my head. I
wasn't scared. I read in the book that if the flame did that it
meant that God was looking over you.

I'm writing this to you grandma because I want you to
know that letting me stay in the back room of your
apartment made me feel so good. it was like you and my
father were with me, but I was alone and I could do what I
wanted at the same time. do you understand? I hope you
do. you helped me so much. I just want you to know that
and that I miss you
and I miss watching tv with you.
I'm still waiting for God to talk to me.
but I feel a little bit better now.

Uncle Gene

My father's name was Eugene.
I was named after him.
He liked to be called Gene.
My father had a younger brother, Frank.
His oldest son Frankie was named after him.
I was nineteen the night my father died.
My mother was out with some friends.
The phone rang at about three o'clock in the morning.
It was my cousin Frankie. I had never spoken
to him on the phone before, so it took me a few seconds
to recognize his voice. It sounded like he was crying.
I asked him if he was ok. He said yeah, he was.
Then he said I have some bad news.
Uncle Gene died.
I said oh man, I'm really sorry.
He didn't say anything else, so I said thanks
for letting me know, and hung up the phone.
I started walking back to my room when I realized
that I didn't have an uncle Gene.

Still Waiting

It was a tall gray building with a ramp and
metal railings on both sides, and lots of little
windows that had yellow curtains on them.

There were two doors in the front of the building.
The first door was made of metal, I think. It was
black or dark brown and it was very thick because
it made this whooshing sound when it opened and
this loud clicking sound when it closed.

There was so much screaming when we got inside.
I had to put my fingers in my ears they hurt so much.
Red and yellow lights kept going on and off and doors
were slamming as tall men carried someone up the stairs
who kept yelling, "Help me! They want to kill me!"

I started to shake as we walked down the hallway.
She held me close to her and I buried my face
in her dress which made me feel a little better.
I didn't want to be there. All I wanted to do was
go home and go back to bed.

I remember riding with them in the ambulance. I didn't
know what time it was but it was dark outside and I
thought there was a fire when she woke me up and told me
to get dressed because I could see red lights flashing
outside my bedroom window and I thought they were from
fire engines. He kept punching himself in the leg saying,
"I'm sorry, I'm sorry," as the ambulance drove through the
streets. I wanted to do something to make him feel better
but I was too scared so I just sat there and looked at him
wishing he would stop. She took his hands in her lap and
started to rub them. "Don't worry, it's not your fault,"

she said. "I know it's not your fault." Then she bent over and kissed me on the head, "My good little boy. My good sweet little boy."

We stopped at one of the doors in the hallway and a man in a long white coat came out and spoke to her then took him inside. I think he was a doctor. I ran over and grabbed his shirt and started pulling him back outside the door until she came over and told me to let go. She said everything was going to be ok. I screamed, "No! I don't want him to go! I don't want him to go!" I kept on screaming as she gently pulled me away from him and brought me to a long wooden bench by a window. We sat down and I put my head on her lap and closed my eyes and she rubbed my back until I fell asleep.

He came home a few days later. When he walked through the front door I ran over to him and gave him the card I made for him at school. I drew a white sanitation truck on the front of the card with garbage cans all around and I drew him in his green sanitation jacket picking up some garbage on the street and people waving to him. Inside the card I wrote "Welcome Home! I Miss You!" His eyes were red and he looked tired. He smiled at me and put the card on the kitchen table then went straight to the bedroom and closed the door. She knocked on the door a few minutes later but he didn't open it. She said something then went into the kitchen, took off her glasses, and put her head down on the kitchen table. It was so quiet I turned on the tv. Then I sat down on the living room couch and waited for them to tell me what was going on but they never did.

Resilience

In all the pictures I have of my mother
before she and my father got divorced,
she had dark brown wavy hair that fell
just below her ears. Her face was
round and smooth and even though she
wore a lot of makeup, you could see she
had a loving, inviting smile, and it was
obvious why my father married her,
even though he told my uncle when they first
started dating that he would never get "hitched,"
no matter how much he liked the girl.

I can't remember when she first started telling me stories
of how they met and how excited she was every time
she saw him but by the time I was eight or nine years old
I knew those stories by heart my favorite one being
when she would bring the phone with her into
the bathroom at two o'clock in the morning
so my grandmother wouldn't hear her talking
to him and she would make plans to meet him
at Junior's Restaurant on Flatbush Avenue in
Brooklyn for breakfast and they would meet
a few hours later after he got off work and before
she had to go to work and when he told me the
same story years later he would say that watching
her walk down the street "all dolled up like that"
made him feel like the luckiest guy in the world.

My grandmother was forty-six when she had my mother
and from the moment she was born my mother knew
that my grandparents never wanted her. My grandfather
rarely spoke to my mother growing up, instead he spent
his free time after work either playing with my aunt and

uncle (my mother's older sister and brother) or fixing things around their apartment, and when my mother would forget just how much he disliked her and ask him for help with something my aunt quickly intervened so that my mother wouldn't have to once again endure the blank loveless stare which was saved just for her, a not-so-gentle reminder of just how unwanted she was.

My grandmother had lost two children about twenty years before my mother was born, and even though she had two other healthy ones a few years later, the indescribable pain which tore through my grandmother's heart always remained with her. But as the years went by and her two living children grew older, the pain lessened a bit until my mother was born, and it was as if the sight of a newborn baby rekindled the agony my grandparents experienced years earlier and no matter how much my mother tried to get them to love her, my grandparents could never forgive her for being born, as she was a constant reminder to them of the devastating cruelty of death that went hand-in-hand with life. And by the time my mother was old enough (seven, maybe eight?) she had no choice but to take on my grandparents' burden of torment and despair and, like them, started hating herself (though she never knew why), wondering why she was ever born in the first place.

My mother was thirty-two when she finally decided to leave my father which was yet another disappointment in the eyes of my grandmother who had actually forgiven my mother for eloping and marrying someone who wasn't Jewish (my father was Italian, which my aunt told me years later was the most tolerable choice the family would accept given the shameful circumstances of my mother choosing a husband outside of her religion), but divorce was almost too much for her to bear, yet somehow after all the wasted years of pain and banishment, my grandmother gradually allowed herself to start to love my mother (as the loneliness of old age started to creep into her life) and, to her credit, despite all the pain and criticism she was forced to endure, my mother welcomed her mother's love with a scarred and open heart.

My parents' marriage quickly disintegrated after I was born, as my father continued to suffer the constant mental anguish of fighting in a war (WWII) that most men from his generation gladly participated in, but had no idea of the effect it would have on some of them years later when they thought the horror of battle was over yet for some it was just beginning, as was the case with my father when the haunting nightmares of bombardment and death weakened and destroyed a once strong and handsome man until he finally gave up and by the time he was forty years old, he was spending most of his days in his pajamas just lying around our one-bedroom apartment, while my mother went to work in Manhattan, reading the newspaper and greeting me at the front door when I got dropped off from school by a neighbor at three o'clock in the afternoon, somehow finding the strength to make me a bologna sandwich and pour me a glass of milk before he went back to sleep, as he desperately tried to hide from the world, and the pain and sadness that constantly consumed him.

By the time I was six my mother finally had enough of the disappointment and misery that awaited her each and every day and took a plane to Texas then a bus to the Mexican border where she crossed over in the middle of the night, a plump, frightened, sad, lonely lost Jewish girl, wondering what she had done so wrong to make life hate her so much. It took six days for her to get a divorce and make it all the way back home to Brooklyn, where she quickly packed our things and took me by the hand, unable to utter even a single word to my father as the realization of what was taking place, the shattering of a dream she so hoped would last a lifetime, was almost too much for her to bear.

And as I blindly followed her down the street to the train station, waving to some of my friends who were just getting out of school, I'll never forget turning my head to look back at my father, his mighty chest heaving with the pain of losing the only two people in the world who he really loved and who really loved him, and as we reached the corner, overcome with emotion and bewilderment, I pulled away from my mother and ran to him as fast as I could, for one more hug, before we left for what I thought was forever.

Those first few years on our own provided little relief for my mother, as all of her time and energy during that frighteningly uncertain time was focused solely on our survival. And everything she did, from sustaining us on only sixty dollars a week, to getting up at five o'clock in the morning just to make me breakfast, to providing me with the safety and security I needed to make my way through the uncharted landscape I was unwittingly thrust into, she did to lessen the pain that continually engulfed me, leaving no room for her to pursue any of the dreams that a thirty-five-year-old single mother was forced to set aside, once again falling victim to a fate that had been cruelly determined for her by some unforeseen malevolent hand.

Things easily could have continued on this way for years, with my mother never fully escaping the damage that had been done to her, routinely going through the motions of a life she never really had a chance to live, were it not for a transformation that slowly began to manifest itself within her as she reached her fortieth birthday. It was around this time that her true self began to finally emerge and take hold of her, giving her the strength and clarity to become the person who she was really meant to be.

*And though many have tried to put this ability? skill? gift?
trait? force? into words, it is an impossible task to
determine why some people are able to overcome the
individual hardships that are thrust upon them, while other
people, sometimes in the exact same circumstances, despite
their best efforts, can never break through the restraints
that force them to live such unfulfilled and stagnant lives.
Fortunately for my mother, the same God (?) that passively
watched as she was tormented by a devastating sadness for
most of her life, was the same God that gave her the
resilience to at times overcome it. But the one question that
will always linger in my mind:* **Why the fuck did He wait
so long?**

This started with her decision to attend Brooklyn College,
where, for the first time in her life, she was introduced to
ways of thinking she had no idea existed, not only through
the courses she took, but by the people she met, people
who were hungry for knowledge and an understanding of a
confused and alienated world, and who embraced
alternative ways of looking at themselves that literally
pushed the boundaries of my mother's consciousness until
she at last started to get a glimpse of who she really was.
And as my mother's transformation continued to take hold,
long-buried feelings started to emerge and make
themselves known to her. At first confused, then
frightened, then enraged at how she had been treated (and
let herself be treated) for most of her life, she gradually
began to acknowledge and embrace these feelings, not as
some new torture that she once again had to endure, but as
a long sought-after remedy in her search to finally become
whole.

My mother's true awakening began about five years later,
when she was finally able to act upon desires that she had
been forced to suppress for such a long and painful time by
the simple-mindedness and cruelty of a society that forced

their biases upon certain groups of people, restricting their right to simply be who they were, and live how they wanted to live, and was welcomed into a community of women—loving, caring, supportive women, women who acknowledged with open and understanding hearts her struggles to simply be who she wanted to be, and provided my mother the opportunity to do so without restraint, judgement, or condemnation. This eventually led to her falling in love with a woman, and for the first time in her life she was able to experience true, meaningful, substantial love, which she both cherished and deserved.

The remaining years of my mother's life alternated between bouts of sadness and moments of joy, yet there were some people who simply could not share in her newfound way of life. And while this caused my mother a great deal of pain, she was eventually able to make an uneasy peace with them, though I had always wished that there would have been a deeper understanding and support for her on their part, as I also wished that there would have been that same understanding and support on her part for them as well, but she refused to let down her walls of protection (understandably so) for fear of what might happen to her if she did.

By the time my mother was in her early sixties, the totality of all that she had been through was beginning to take its toll on her. Her day-to-day existence had become a burden that was almost too much for her to bear. She had been out of work for nearly ten years, as the job market was not welcoming to someone her age. She did go on some interviews, but in the end they all turned out to be fruitless. This was a tremendous blow to my mother's self-worth, which led to her isolating herself from her friends and family, and even from the woman she loved. Despite this, that same unexplainable resiliency which helped my mother make it this far once again nudged her forward, and she applied for a special work program in which she had to take a number of tests (she was a supervising bookkeeper) and complete various assignments, along with mandatory interviews. The entire process took nearly two months, and three days before she died she was accepted into the program. More than just a job opportunity, getting into this program not only validated my mother's forty-year work career, it also validated who she was as a person; strong, unyielding, unflinching, and always able to make other people feel better about themselves, no matter how much pain she was in. And I just want the world to know that.

Her Secret

I liked sleeping over
my aunt's house
with the big willow tree
in the backyard
and the little red tomatoes
growing in bunches
near the glass door to the
basement. she would let me
taste them but only one or two
at a time and only if
they were red,
not yellow or green
and she would tell me to wash
them off with the hose that came
out of the back wall of her house
but most of the time I just cleaned
them off with my fingers and popped
them in my mouth, they tasted
so sweet and so delicious.

I woke up one morning and
went downstairs to the kitchen
to get a drink of water when I
saw her by the sink making
coffee and I started to tip-toe
over to surprise her but she
heard me coming and she
turned around and wiped her
hands on her flowered apron and
knelt down and hugged me
and kissed me on the cheek
and after I kissed her back she
asked me if I was feeling ok and
I said yes and that all I wanted
was a glass of water and she said

how about I make you something
special to drink. I smiled and said
sure, and she said great I just have
to get a few things so I went over
to the kitchen table and pulled a chair
out for her when she brought over
two glasses, a container of milk,
a long silver spoon, and a jar of
Ovaltine. we used to have Ovaltine
at our house but I didn't like it
because after you put the chocolate
powder in the glass and filled it up
with milk, no matter how fast
you stirred it there would always
be some powder left on top of
the milk and when you drank it
the powder would get stuck in your
teeth or you would swallow it in
little clumps and it tasted horrible
so we switched to Bosco which was
really just thick chocolate syrup and
even though Ovaltine tasted better
than Bosco we stuck with Bosco
because no one wanted to scrape off
the clumps of Ovaltine from the top
of the glass every time you made
chocolate milk.

she saw the look on my face as she put
two spoons of Ovaltine in one of the
glasses and laughed and said don't
worry about the clumps (how did she
know about the clumps? I thought) I'm
going to show you the secret to making
the best glass of chocolate milk
you ever had…without the clumps.
I leaned over the kitchen table

to get a closer look at what she was
doing and watched as she poured
a little bit of milk into the glass,
just enough to cover the Ovaltine
and then she started mixing it
together really really fast with the
longs silver spoon until all of the Ovaltine
was gone and all that was left was
this brownish gooey stuff at the bottom
of the glass and she laughed again
when she saw my face
and said don't worry (but I did anyway)
then she filled the rest of the glass up
with milk and mixed that up with the
gooey brown stuff and I couldn't
believe it but when she was done
mixing there were no clumps
of Ovaltine in the milk
and it was smooth and dark brown
just like Bosco and when I drank it
I didn't taste any powder and nothing
got stuck in my teeth and it was so delicious
that I finished the glass in one big
gulp and just looked at my aunt
and wondered what other secrets
did she know.

keys

the nights
that
you went out

you let me
sleep
in your bed

and I
would lie
awake

until
I heard
the sound
of your keys

unlocking
the front door

Jelly Apples

I knew she was having a bad day because she didn't answer the phone when I called her, and when I went over to see her, she wouldn't open the door when I knocked. I could hear her walking around inside of her apartment, so I said through the door that I wanted to take her to Coney Island, so she could walk on the beach and dip her feet in the water, which was one of her favorite things to do. She opened the door a few minutes later. Her eyes were red and her long wavy brownish-gray hair was crumbled up in a ball like she had just gotten out of bed. It was around three in the afternoon. "I'll be ready in a few minutes," she said. Then she quickly closed the door behind her. We didn't say a word to each other on the car ride over, but when we got to the beach, and were walking in the sand, she finally started talking. "We used to spend the whole day here in the summer when I was little. Me, your aunt, and your uncle. Your grandmother would give us each a quarter, which was enough for the train, three rides, and lunch. I remember we had so much fun I didn't want to go home." We walked a little while longer, then left the beach and started walking on the boardwalk. We passed by a hot dog stand and I bought two hot dogs and two large cups of orange soda. It was crowded on the boardwalk, and we sat down on two benches that faced the ocean. After a few minutes she took off her glasses and started to cry. I asked her what was wrong. She hesitated, then said, "He used to tease me all the time, and no one ever told him to stop." For years my mother would tell me stories of how my uncle used to tease her when she was a young girl, and how much she begged him to stop but he never did. I usually just tuned her out, but today, for some reason, I asked her what he did to her that was so terrible. She looked at me with such sadness. "He used to pinch me and pull my hair. Sometimes he would sit on top of me until I couldn't breathe. Then he would hide my glasses and laugh at me when I couldn't find them." I looked at her and shook my head. "That's it? That's all he did was sit on you and pull your hair and hide your glasses? What's the big deal? Every brother does that to his little sister. You're almost fifty years old. You have to stop letting little things like that bother you." All of a sudden, my mother stood up, threw her cup of orange soda in my face, and started screaming at me, "You selfish bastard! You have no idea what it was like being picked on like that every day! Every single fuckin' day! It was horrible!" I could feel the soda running down my face. People started laughing at me as I tried to wipe some of it off with my hands. I wanted to say something to my mother, but she had already left. I ran after her shouting, "I'm sorry. I'm sorry. I didn't mean it. Please stop. I'm sorry." My mother turned around and screamed back at me, "Leave me alone! Just leave me the fuck alone!" Some guy said something to her and I told him to mind his fuckin' business. I was starting to get really pissed. "Would you just stop already?" I shouted. "You're acting like a little kid." My mother started walking towards me. "Don't tell me what the fuck to do! You're not my father." Then I just lost it. "Well maybe if you acted your age, not like some fuckin' eight-year-old girl, I wouldn't have to act like your father." My mother mumbled something at me I couldn't understand then started to walk away. I kept on following her until she sat down on one of the benches and lit a cigarette. I stood there watching her, thinking how all alone she looked. I should have just kept my fuckin' mouth shut, I thought. I didn't know what to do. Then I saw a man walking by selling jelly apples. I remembered how much my mother loved eating them, and how much it made her laugh when I would get some of the caramel stuck between my teeth and how my fingers would turn red when I tried to pull the pieces of apple out of my mouth. I bought two of them and sat down next to her on the bench. I asked her if she wanted one the apples. She didn't say anything, she just looked at me and took one. After a few bites, she got up and started walking back to the beach. I followed her and together we walked down to the water and stayed there until it got dark. Then we walked back to the car and I drove her home. I know she tried, but she just couldn't forget any of it.

Abandoned

When my father was forty-eight years old, he started dating a woman (girl) who was twenty-two. He was working as a maître d' in a restaurant in Manhattan called The Inner Circle. It was upscale, with a long bar and a piano player that played there every Friday and Saturday night. I don't know the details of how my father and this girl met, but within a month or two, not only were they dating, but they were living together. I was thirteen at the time, and really didn't pay much attention to the age difference between them. The only thing that upset me was the fact that my father started seeing me less and less, until he stopped seeing me completely (it would be over nine months before I saw him again at my cousin's wedding, and even then, it was *me* who went over to *him*). I know that devastated me beyond comprehension, but I can't feel how I felt about it anymore (which, I think, is a good thing) perhaps because I have done everything that I can to block out the unbearable pain it caused me. The only tangible thing I have left from that very sad and traumatic time in my life was a letter I wrote and mailed to my father, about two months after he stopped seeing me. I never received a reply.

May 18th, 1972

Dear Dad,

I didn't want to write this letter to you but my mother said that I should write it because you should know how I am feeling right now. It has been over two months since you stopped picking me up and seeing me. I am very mad at you. The last time I saw you we went to the movies and you said that you had to go to the bathroom but you didn't come back for two hours and I had to watch the movie all by myself. I know you were on the phone with her. You can talk to her anytime you want to. Why did you have to call her when you were with me? I only see you one time a week. That is not a lot. I miss you very much. Do you miss me at all? It's not right that you see her and you don't see me. You promised me that if you ever have a girlfriend, you would still see me on the weekends, but now you stopped seeing me because of her. And you never told me why. I still love you but I don't want to see you anymore until you stop being with her. She told me one night when you were working that she doesn't like me. She said it was my fault you got sick and went to the hospital and that you would feel better if you didn't see me anymore. I didn't make you go to the hospital. I'm your son. I wouldn't do that to you. I hope you know that. I love you. I don't want to make you feel bad but I think of you every day and I'm very sad that you don't want to see me anymore. When we went bowling she came with us. I didn't want to go because she was going. You said it was just going to be me and you. Why did she have to come with us? I said I wanted a soda when we were at the bowling alley but I went to the phone booth and called my mother and told her how mad I was that she was with us. I told her that I wanted to come home early. She said that you still loved me. I don't think you do. Why won't you see me anymore? I hate your girlfriend so much. I don't want to see her again. I love you more than she does. She is too young for you anyway. She is only nine years older than me. I don't want this letter to upset you but you upset me. I hope you are feeling good. I never want you to go to the hospital again. When you read this letter please call me. If you forgot my phone number it is 718-871-5710. I wrote this letter all by myself.

Your Son. Eugene

Not Forgetting Him

On those nights when she felt like talking
she'd ask if I could stay a little longer
and we'd sit around the kitchen table
she'd light a cigarette and start to cry
then say how much I looked like him
she'd lean over and touch my cheek
her hands trembling I'd take them in mine
and kiss them while under her breath
she'd start telling me of the first time
she met him he was so handsome
then she'd turn away and wipe her glasses
and kiss my hands and rub them against her cheeks
her face red and full of tears

I remember his shirt she went on pressed and white
it smelled like spring he bent down and kissed me
my face buried deep inside of his chest it was so big
we danced for hours until no one was left just us
and when we were done, he held the door open
and we walked outside the streets so busy
filled with people but all I saw was him
and when he called the next night and asked me
to meet him after work I was so happy I couldn't
breathe it was three in the morning when I got there
I ran to him out of breath he picked me up
and swung me around and laughed when I kissed him
and told him that I couldn't sleep the night before
I could only think of him then we walked a few blocks
and had breakfast I couldn't stop looking at him
I was tired but I didn't want to close my eyes
not for a second not while he was so close to me
it was almost six in the morning when I got home
my face pressed against the kitchen window
I watched him drive away
waving long after he was gone

he called again the next night
I sat in the bathroom with the phone on my lap
whispering so no one would hear
we talked for hours about what I can't remember
I just remember him
his voice
his face
his smile his cheeks
his hands
the way he looked whenever he saw me
I miss him
I know. I miss him too

It's almost eleven she walks me to the door
thanks me for staying so late kisses my forehead
then takes my face in her hands kisses me again
and tells me how much I look like him
the lines in her face etched with years of sadness
I wait until she locks the door
and listen to her fading footsteps
the kitchen light goes out
she mumbles something
I laugh and call out good night
then take the elevator down
to the first floor

I walk to the corner where he used to meet me
no matter how early I got up
he was always there waiting for me
with his big wide smile I would run to him
out of breath he would pick me up
and swing me around until I stopped crying
then he would laugh as he wiped his face
and walked me to his car so early in the morning
no one else around the empty streets clear and long
my eyes on him the whole time as he pulled away
his hand resting on my knee

I played with his fingers
kissed them one by one
singing silly made-up songs
of pirate ships and monster dragons
he took my face in his hand
and held it there brushed back my hair
rubbed my cheek and asked me
where I wanted to go
with you I said
I want to go with you

I stared down the street empty by now
it's almost midnight, I wonder what to do
when I realize there's really only one thing
to do so I go back up to her apartment
she's still awake when I knock on the door
she smiles and gives me a blanket and a pillow
I fall asleep on the couch
the next morning when I wake up
I see her making breakfast
my clothes neatly folded beside me
I take my seat at the kitchen table
nothing really to say we just smile and wonder
what it would have been like
to have him around just a little bit longer
then make plans for next week

Realization

we went outside
for the first time
since he left
the hospital
after his second
heart attack

he was barely able
to stand on his own.
I held his arm
which was soft
like a rubber hose
as he scraped his feet
along the sidewalk
slowly inching forward
like a beaten old man
even though he was
only 51 years old

he had to stop
after half a block
to catch his breath.
his face sunken in,
his body depleted
from years of pain
and neglect

he held onto a wire
fence for balance
when a friend of his
saw him and came over
to say hello

as they shook hands,

the veins in my father's
fingers filled up with blood
as he tried to muster up
enough strength to hide
the fact of his decline

they spoke for a while
and after his friend left
I was about to ask
my father how he was feeling
but the look on his face
said it all:

I'd rather be dead
than ever be seen
like this again

dial tone

she told me that
when she first
left my father
and we moved
into our apartment
every night
she would pick up the receiver
and listen for a dial tone
to see if the phone was working
because no one ever called her

I can't imagine
being that lonely

Pete Rose

The first summer I went
to sleepaway camp I was
nine years old and you
dropped me off where
the buses were parked
and you waited with all
of the other parents until
they checked our bags and
gave us our bus numbers
and as I started to walk to my bus
with all of the other kids I saw you
standing there and I ran off the line
and through the crowd of parents and
when I found you, you bent down and
hugged me and said don't worry I'll be
waiting for you right here when you come back
in two weeks and that made me feel good until
I got on the bus and it started to pull away and I
couldn't see you anymore and I realized just how
much I was going to miss you

It was a long bus ride through the streets
of the city then onto a highway that led
to a big bridge and after we crossed over it
we drove on another highway with trees
and grass on both sides and then the bus
started going up and down hills which was
like a roller coaster and we even passed by
a lake with sailboats on it and even though
I had never been on a sailboat before it looked
like fun and the bus kept going for I really don't
know how long until one of the kids shouted:
"we're almost there!" and some of the other kids
started clapping but some of the other kids started
booing which made me a little confused so I didn't

clap *or* boo I just sat there looking out of the window
hoping that the next two weeks would go by very fast.

When we finally got to the camp, we got off the bus
and the counselors called out our names and told us
which cabin we were going to be in but before we went
there we all went to this long building called the dining
hall and we sat on benches on either side of a wooden
table and the waiters (who were around fourteen or fifteen
years old) gave us tuna fish sandwiches and chocolate milk
for lunch then ice cream cones for dessert and the tuna fish
sandwiches were ok but they weren't as good as you made
them with chopped celery and onions and thin slices of
tomatoes with just a little bit of mayonnaise to keep it all
together but I was so hungry from the long bus ride that I
ate the sandwich anyway, and when we were done with
lunch we picked up our bags and went to our cabins and
some of the kids started talking to each other (I guess
because they went to camp together last year but nobody
talked to me because this was my first time here) and I
started to think about all of my friends back home and I
wondered what they were doing maybe they were playing
punchball or tag in the schoolyard and I started to miss
them and I wished that I was playing with them too and
when we got to our cabin we chose which bed we wanted
to sleep on then our counselors gave us index cards and we
wrote our names on them and taped them to the front of our
beds and after we put our clothes away in these little cubby
holes next to our bed we went outside and played soccer on
this big grass field and even though I can't run too fast I
can kick a soccer ball pretty far and I almost scored a goal
and one of the kids on my team said nice shot which made
me feel good and I told him my name and he told me his
and I told him I was from Brooklyn and he told me he was
from Queens but we still could be friends which made me
laugh, then we went back to our cabin to rest up a little
before we went down to the lake for our swimming test and

when I got to my bed, I saw that there were two white
envelopes on my pillow and I thought that someone made a
mistake but when I picked them up, they had my name on
them and I recognized your handwriting right away and I
got so excited that I ripped open the first envelope and little
pieces of newspaper went flying out all over the place and
the kid in the bed next to me picked them up and gave
them to me and one of them said The New York Post
Sports Page across the top then underneath it, "Pete Rose
gets five hits in Saturday's game against the Dodgers" and
there was a letter inside the envelope and it said that you
didn't know if they had any newspapers at the
sleepaway camp I was going to and you thought you'd
send me some newspaper clippings of my favorite baseball
player, Pete Rose, so I wouldn't miss anything while I was
away and when I picked up the second envelope some of
the kids sat down on my bed (they didn't ask me, but that
was ok) and when I opened it, it also had a few newspaper
clippings about Pete Rose but this one was from The
Daily News and it also had The Jumble in it (which we
always did together when you took me for the weekend)
and then I read your letter which said that when I came
home you would take me to my favorite pizza place in
Astoria, Queens and I could order one of their small pies
with mushrooms on it, and I started to get hungry again
when one of the kids asked me if I needed some help with
the Jumble and I said "sure," then the rest of the kids
started to gather around me, some standing, some sitting on
the cubby next to my bed and one of the kids asked me
why I liked Pete Rose so much and I told him because he
was your favorite player plus he was a switch hitter which
made it harder for a pitcher to strike him out and he had a
cool nickname, "Charlie Hustle," because he always ran as
hard as he could during a game no matter what the score
was then one kid said his favorite player was Bob Gibson
because he could throw a baseball over one hundred miles
an hour and I said yeah my father told me about him he

pitches for the St. Louis Cardinals, and the kid said yeah, you're right, and then all of the other kids started talking about their favorite baseball players and other stuff and I held your letter in my hand and it was like you were sitting right there next to me

Some Things Never Change

we met again after fifty years
fifty years, a lifetime
there were marriages
and children, later on grandchildren
even one great-grandchild
who would ever have imagined that
back in 1972?

fifty years of days melting into one another
falling over each other like dominos
we would meet up with not much to say
it was more just seeing each other
than anything else
the relief of knowing
that you were real
and yesterday
was not a dream
I made up
to comfort myself

we immediately started running
running running running
screaming falling pushing pulling
we would spend the day
in hilarious joy never really understanding
what was going on or how much we all meant
to each other but instead, just seven or eight
once random atoms suddenly drawn to one another
colliding into one another
energizing one another
comforting one another
reinforcing one another
loving one another
and on and on it went
day after day, hour after hour

just us while the world went
on, taking very little notice
which was just the way we liked it
and when we met again
all those years later
yes, we were older
yes, we were feebler
yes, time was etched in our faces
but that feeling
that glorious feeling that held us together
was still there
and as I looked across the table at all of you
there you were
like it was
like it will always be

you want to know what love is?
after you read this put on your jacket
and walk to the nearest park or empty lot
or schoolyard and watch those atoms
continue to collide

their gift to me

I never
got
the chance
to say
goodbye
to either
of them
before
they died

I think
they
wanted it
that way

Soap and Warm Water

One Sunday night after my father dropped me off we met on the steps of the bank where we used to hang out and after a few minutes I could tell something was going on because everybody was laughing but no one would tell me what they were laughing at so I asked them and they still wouldn't tell me what they were laughing at which got me pretty mad until Jimmy finally said that they found this place in the city where you can have sex with a girl for only ten dollars and I said no way and Chris said yeah we went there last night after Gus came around and told us about this place called the Intimate Room where all you had to do was pay ten dollars and you got this big round coin and then you went downstairs where there were about twenty girls sitting in a circle and you picked the one that you liked and gave her the coin and she would take you to a room and let you have sex with her and I said you couldn't wait for me to go there and have sex too and Chris said we wanted to wait for you but Gus was going there and we thought he could take us because we might get lost on the train plus none of us wanted to be virgins anymore so we went with him and now none of us *are* virgins anymore except for you then everybody started laughing again but I was too busy thinking about how I was going to get ten dollars to be mad at them and a couple of days later after I took out most of the change I had in this big glass jar in my room and rolled up all the coins and brought them to the bank and I had just enough money to go and I asked Jimmy to show me where the place was and we took the train into the city and got off at 42nd street and walked a few blocks until we got there and I paid ten dollars to a guy behind a glass window with a hole in it like they have at the movies and he gave me a coin like Chris said he would and Jimmy asked if he could come in and sit down and just look at the girls because he didn't have any money and the guy said are you nuts so Jimmy said he would wait for me on the corner then I walked down the stairs and went inside and I was really nervous because I had never done anything like this before I mean I dreamed of doing something like this before but I always thought that the first girl I would do it with would be Sheila Wolf because I had a crush on her since first grade but she liked Michael Gray more than me and just like the guys said there were about twenty girls sitting in a circle and I started looking at all of them trying to figure out which one I wanted to have sex with when another guy who worked there said "let's go pick one already we haven't got all day" so I gave my coin to the first girl that I thought looked pretty and she had long blonde hair with silver earrings and a silver necklace and she was wearing this red bathing suit with a black belt around it and black boots and she smiled at me when I gave her the coin then she took my hand and we walked down this long hallway with disco music playing and red lights blinking on and off until we stopped at this room which had pictures of naked girls on the door in all different positions some of them I had never seen before and when I went inside the room she asked me what would I like to do and I didn't know what to say so I said I'd like to have sex with you and she smiled and said ok honey that's what I'm here for then she told me to take off my pants and walk over to this sink that was at the back of the room so she could wash my penis and I told her that my penis was clean already because I took a shower this morning before I came here like I always do and she laughed and said that she believed me but she had to be sure so I walked over to the sink and she turned on the water and it was warm then she put some soap in her hands and asked me to lean over the sink and she took my penis in her hands and started rubbing it up and down and it felt really good with the soap and warm water all over it and it was the first time that a girl had ever touched my penis and she kept on rubbing it up and down and it felt even better when her fingers started moving all around and she even started washing my testicles which I thought was pretty weird because you don't have sex with your testicles you have sex with your penis when all of a sudden she screamed out "no, no, not yet honey not yet" but I couldn't help it and it just started coming out all over her fingers and hands and it wouldn't stop some of it even squirted on the side of the sink and I said I was sorry and that I didn't mean to do it and she laughed and said that's ok honey but next time make sure you wait until I'm done cleaning it and then she kissed me on the cheek and gave me a towel and I wiped myself off then put my pants on and after I walked back up the stairs I saw Jimmy waiting for me on the corner and he said so how does it feel not to be a virgin anymore and I said it felt great, then we took the train home and about a week later I went back there by myself and after I paid the ten dollars to the same guy behind the glass window I walked down the stairs and saw the same girl as last week and she was wearing the same red bathing suit but this time she had on a brown belt and brown boots and I went right over to her and gave her my coin and we went to the same room but I didn't have to wait for her to tell me to take off my pants only when I got to the sink I said could you please use cold water this time.

Gay

I couldn't stop thinking about how she wasn't like any of my mother's other friends. She was nice to me and sometimes she was funny, but she was different from my mother. She was big and rough-looking and had short hair and always wore big blue rolled-up dungarees with a thick black belt, and work boots. I thought it was really weird. My mother didn't dress that way. She always dressed nice and neat, but lately she stopped wearing makeup and cut her hair pretty short and she also stopped wearing dresses to work all the time. I just couldn't understand why my mother was hanging out with her so much instead of her other friends, the ones that I liked. And why did she have to sleep over all the time? I stayed in my room most of the time she came over because I didn't want to see her which got pretty boring and I couldn't go in the living room to watch tv because she would probably be there. It was really starting to bother me. I walked into the kitchen to get something to eat and saw my mother sitting there having a cup of coffee, and for some reason the thought just popped into my head and I said, "Hey ma, is Vicki gay?" She didn't say anything, she just sat there, looking at me, and I knew right away something was up so I asked her again "Hey ma, is Vicki gay?" She hesitated for a few seconds then said "Does it matter if she is or not?" By now I was starting to get annoyed (all I wanted was a simple answer) so I said "Please, ma, just answer the question. Is Vicki gay or not?" She put her coffee cup down, got up from her chair, and slowly started walking towards me. She paused for a couple of seconds then said, "Yes, honey, Vicki is gay." "I knew it!" I said, proud of myself for some reason. And then she said "What does that mean?" and I said "Well, look at her. She's so big and she's not really good looking or anything. I mean look at the way she dresses with those rolled-up dungarees and work-boots. Even her voice doesn't sound like a girl's voice." I could tell that

94

really upset my mother but I didn't realize just how much until she said I had no right to say those things about Vicki. "Well, it's ok to say them if they're true, right?" I said. "I mean the truth is the truth, isn't it? I don't even know why you hang around with her anyway. Your other friends are so much nicer than she is." That really pissed my mother off. "What I do and who I choose to do it with is none of your business. You're just a child. You don't know anything about me or what makes me happy. Vicki is my friend and I like being with her. That's all you need to know." I started screaming at her, "I'm not a child! I'm fifteen years old and I can say what I want to say and I'm saying I hate Vicki. She's big and fat and ugly. She's disgusting." Then I turned around and started walking to the front door before my mother could say anything else when I suddenly thought to myself, "Well if Vicki's gay and she sleeps in the same bed as my mother and they hang out together all the time, and they're going away together next weekend then that must mean…oh shit…no…no … fuck…no…she must be gay too…My mother's gay! My fuckin' mother is gay!" I never thought of my mother being gay before. I thought some of her new friends who looked and acted like Vicki *might* be gay or a lesbian or something but I never thought that *my* mother would ever be gay. She didn't look like them or act like them…she was pretty and she liked men…she even married my father and had a kid…it didn't make any sense to me but the thoughts just kept coming faster and faster…the Playboy magazines I found in the back of the kitchen cabinet, the tv show she made me watch with her about a divorced guy who introduces his son to his boyfriend…the fact that it had been a couple of years since she brought a guy to the apartment, and then things started to fit together and I turned back around and looked at her and started screaming: "You're gay too, right ma? Right? You're gay like Vicki, right? Fuck! You're fuckin' gay! I can't believe it…you're a fuckin' gay fuckin' lesbian. Fuck! Why do *you* have to be gay? Why? Why the fuck does all this shit have to happen to me? Why me? Fuck. I didn't do anything to anybody!" My mother started walking towards me and I told her to stay the fuck away from me and she screamed at me with tears running down her face, "Don't you ever talk to me like that again, do you hear me!" Then she tried to hit me but I grabbed her hand and screamed back at her, "Fuck you. You're fuckin' gay. Fuck man another fuckin' thing about me that's all fucked up. It wasn't enough that you got divorced or I didn't have any brothers or sisters like everyone else does. You had to be gay too! Didn't you? DIDN'T YOU!" "Shut up. Just shut up!" she screamed back at me. "What the hell do you know anyway? Nothing. You don't know anything about me or what I need. I care about Vicki and she cares about me! Do you hear me! She cares about me and I'm not going to let you shit all over that!" Then she tried to hit me again but I moved out of the way. I had never seen her so angry before. I was a little scared. We both just stood there in the hallway looking at each other. I really didn't know what was happening. My chest was heaving. I was shaking all over. I had a hard time breathing. I took a step towards her. "Stay away from me," she said. "Just stay the hell away from me." Then she went back into the kitchen, sat down at the table, lit a cigarette, and started sobbing in her hands. I didn't know what to do, so I turned around and walked out the front door and just started wandering around, lost in a place I had never been before.

The Bus Ride Home

It was only when it was time to leave
and we were standing by their front door
bundled up in our coats and scarves
like two lost starving orphans
begging for someone to give us a ride home
that I started to realize
what it felt like to be nothing,
cast aside, invisible, meaningless,
more alone than I ever imagined
anyone could ever be.

Everyone else there was married.
Everyone else there had cars.
Everyone else there had money.
Everyone else there lived in a real home
instead of a one-bedroom apartment
with paper thin walls and mice that
scurried around in the middle of the night.
Everyone else there felt safe.
Everyone else there felt cared for.
Everyone else there had normal lives.

But us?
We didn't have any of that.
We *never* had any of that.
All we had was each other.
Why?
What did we do to deserve this?
It didn't matter.
All that mattered
was the feeling of negation
that rose up inside of us
as we saw everyone
hugging each other
smiling, happy

knowing that the darkness
that was waiting outside to swallow us up
would never, ever, dare to come near them.

And as each person walked past us
I watched her face slowly change
from joyous acceptance to devastating rejection,
their unspoken words tearing us apart:
you're inferior
you're separate
you're different
you're less than
you're an embarrassment
you're undeserving
you're worthless
you're forgotten
you're discarded
you're a joke
you're inhuman
you're not like us
you'll *never* be like us

Moments before they would laugh with you,
cry with you, hug you, kiss you,
tell you how much they loved you
but now, when you needed them the most
when you needed their protection
their understanding, their caring
they tossed you aside, ignored you
as if you never existed,
your usefulness coming to an end
like a box of Christmas ornaments
you pack away and shove in the
back of your closet, far out of sight
until you need them
and then, and *only* then
do you bring them out into the light

for all the world to see.

What was she thinking?
watching them leave together
relishing another event-filled night
they would recall weeks later
over drinks at some fancy restaurant
as the darkness loomed outside
ready to swallow us up.

How could they not see us standing there
RIGHT IN FRONT OF THEM!
were they all so blind?
a single mother and her eight-year-old son
leaving the warmth and security of a real home,
full of movement, full of life,
forced to walk alone
in the silent darkness,
the cold, menacing, heartless darkness
waiting in anticipation for another victim
to descend upon and devour.

Did she hate them?
I was too young to hate them
but now I'm consumed
with a hatred matched only by the agony
I saw in her face as they turned on
the ignition to their cars, the hum
of their engines reverberating
mercilessly in our ears as they slowly,
comfortably drove through the same streets
we were left standing in, waiting for a bus
we hoped would come and take us home

It was dark when we finally left their house

and I started to get a little scared
as we walked down the empty streets
to the bus stop.
I reached up to hold my mother's hand,
not really knowing if it was to comfort
me or to comfort her.

"Why do we always have to take the bus home?" I asked.
"Because everyone's car is filled up."
"No they're not. There were two empty seats in Uncle
___'s car, and T___ drove here by himself. I know because
I saw him get out of his car when I was playing outside."
She didn't say anything.
"Why don't you have a car like everyone else does? My
father has a car. If he were here, he would drive us home."
I was too young to realize just how much that upset her.
"Can I give the dimes to the bus driver this time?"
"That's your job, isn't it," she managed to say.
"Don't worry. I'm going to get a car really soon," I said.
"Then we won't have to take the bus anymore
and I can drive you anywhere you want to go. I promise."
She turned her head and started to cry.
"Where do you want to go?" I asked her.
"What?" she said, distracted.
"Where do you want to go when I get my car? I want to go
to the park in Queens where my father takes me. It's called
Juniputer Volley Park."
She started to laugh.
"It's called Juniper *Valley* Park."
"How did you know that? Did you ever go there
with my father before we left?"
She took a deep breath.
"I used to go there with your father a lot."
"Did you ever play handball with him? I play handball
with him all the time but we use paddles because my
hands
are too small to hit the ball."

"I think we might have played handball once or twice,"
she said.
"Really? Did you beat him?"
"Of course I beat him," she smilcd.
"No you didn't."
She bent down and hugged me. "You bet I did."
We both started to laugh.
"Don't worry, soon my hands will be big enough
and I'll beat him for you."
The bus finally came a few minutes later,
and after we sat down she leaned her head
on my shoulder and fell asleep.

And for a while, all of it was forgotten.

Until the next time.

––––––––––––––––––

Once, when I was sixteen, we came late to someone's
surprise birthday party. We had to take the train all the way
to Long Island. It took us almost three hours. Then we had
to take a cab from the train station to their house. It was
hot. I was hungry. I was pissed. We had relatives at the
party who lived in Brooklyn but not one of them offered us
a ride. Not one. When we got there I heard someone say,
"She's always late. Why doesn't she…" "Why doesn't she
what?" I yelled across the room. "Get here on time?
Because she doesn't drive. That's why WE didn't get here
on time!" Everyone was looking at me. "What? How
about somebody offering to pick us up from the fuckin'
train station. One time. Just one fuckin' time." I was
looking straight at the guy. I didn't even know who he was.
I wanted to fuckin' kill him. "Why don't you control your
son," he said to my mother. That put me over the edge.
"I'm right here," I screamed back at him. "You have

something to say, say it to me." My mother started to cry. I didn't realize how much I upset her. But I didn't care. Nobody ever says anything to anybody about any of this. The guy smiled at me. I started walking towards him. "What's so funny asshole?" My cousin ran over to me. "I'm tired of this," I said to him. "The same shit happens every fuckin' time we have to go somewhere." He hugged me. I started to cry. "It's not fair man. It's not fuckin' fair." He walked me outside. We sat down by this little pond they had in their backyard. "I'm not going back in there," I said. "I'll kill that fuckin' guy. I swear to God I'll rip his fuckin' head off." "Ok. Ok. So we'll stay out here." I started to cry again. "It just sucks, you know. The whole fuckin' thing just sucks." "I know it does," he said. "I know."

Fat Fish and Turtle Boy

most days when he dropped me off
I would walk right past her
and go straight to my room
and just sit on my bed
trying not to think of how much I missed him
and after a while I would come out
and she would ask me how the weekend went
and what I wanted for lunch
and I would sit down at the kitchen table
and she would make me a sandwich
of turkey and tomato and mustard
and sit across from me
and in between bites I would tell her
of all the things we did
and she would smile

but on other days
I would just stay in my room
and sit on my bed
and think of him driving home
and how I held his face in my hands
when he picked me up
to kiss me goodbye
tracing the curves of his cheeks
on my blanket
until she knocked on my door
and asked if I was hungry
but I wouldn't answer her
and she would leave me alone
because she knew

and when she finally came back
a few hours later
she would open the door
this time without knocking

and find me hiding under my desk
with my chin between my knees
and my hands over my head
and she would tip-toe across the floor
taking big deep breaths as she went
until her cheeks swelled up
and she would push her lips out
and place her hands behind her ears
spreading her fingers out
until they almost covered her cheeks
and she would brush them back and forth
moving her head from side to side
then get down on her knees
and whisper just loud enough
for me to hear

"Here comes Fat Fish
swimming in the sea
the beautiful deep blue sea
looking for someone to play with"

and she would crawl across the floor
in all different directions
her eyes moving back and forth
making funny noises with her nose
until I stuck my head out just a bit
then pulled it back in when she saw me

"There is someone to play with
There is someone to play with Fat Fish
Turtle Boy, won't you play with Fat Fish?
Won't you play with Fat Fish
in the beautiful deep blue sea?"

I could hear her moving towards me

with each word that she said
but I wouldn't answer her
only a few minutes later
I would stick my head out again
to see where she was
then pull it back in
when I felt her
getting closer

"Turtle Boy come out and play
Come out and play with Fat Fish
Come and swim past the red and blue fish
and the yellow rocks shining in the sun
Come Turtle Boy, come play with Fat Fish
in the beautiful deep blue sea
She is very lonely? Are you lonely too?"

then she would stop and it would be quiet
and I would sit there wiping my eyes
thinking of the sea
and what it would be like
to swim past red and blue fish
and feel the warm water
brush up against my face

and I would sit there
waiting for her to say something
but she wouldn't say anything
so I would stick my head out
to see where she was
but when I looked
she wasn't there
so I would stick my head out a little further
thinking that I would see her
but she still wasn't there
so I inched my way out
from under my desk

hoping to see where she was
but no matter where I looked
she wasn't there

then all of a sudden
from behind my bookcase
I saw her big fat cheeks
and long black hair
hanging over her shoulders
and she was smiling
as she came crawling towards me

"Turtle Boy here is Fat Fish
waiting for you to swim with her
in the beautiful deep blue sea
Don't be afraid, Turtle Boy
Fat Fish will take care of you
Fat Fish will always take care of you"

then I slowly got up on my hands and knees
and inched my way out from under my desk
and followed her out the door
thinking of him and smiling
as we passed by
the red and blue fish
swimming beside us

Second in Command

I was around nine or ten when I started sleeping over my uncle's house on the weekends my father didn't take me. At first I thought I did something to upset my mother, that's why she didn't want to be with me, but when I got older I realized just how hard it was for her to do everything by herself, especially when she had me to take care of, so I understood if she wanted to do something by herself every once in a while.

During the week my mother would get up early in the morning, around five o'clock, to make me breakfast and help me get ready for school. Then she would take the train into Manhattan and work all day sometimes to six o'clock at night when she would take the train back home to Brooklyn, getting pushed and shoved by all of the other people riding on the train with her. When she finally made it home she had to make me dinner and twice a week she would do laundry and even though I helped her she still had to load up our wagon with clothes and laundry detergent and walk about eight blocks to the laundromat because the washer and dryer in the basement of our apartment building never worked and while I went to bed around nine o'clock I could still hear her walking around our apartment doing things I didn't even know had to be done.

On the weekends I slept over his house, I would meet my uncle at his store on Friday afternoons after school, and I would sit in the back of his office and do my homework while he talked to customers on the phone and doodled in this yellow notepad that he kept in one of the drawers of his long wooden desk and he would draw all kinds of shapes like squares and triangles and octagons (the first time I ever saw an octagon was on one of his yellow notepads) with perfectly lined edges that he would shade in with his pencil and all the shapes crisscrossed over each other so many times that you couldn't tell what shape they really were anymore and I always knew when he had a really tough customer because he would sharpen his pencil and start a new page of doodles.

It was about a forty-minute ride from my uncle's store to his house and as we drove through the streets of Brooklyn, he would ask me these really weird questions, some of which I couldn't understand because he was so smart and I guess because he thought that I was smart too.

One time when he had to work late, we didn't leave his store until around six-thirty. It was dark outside and there was a full moon, and as we walked to his car he asked me which was bigger the moon or my hand. I said that was easy, the moon, of course. He just stood there smiling at me (which wasn't a good sign). "Are you sure?" he asked me. "Of course I'm sure," I said. Then he told me to lift up my right hand a few inches in front of my face. "Can you see the moon now?" he asked me. "No," I said. "Of course not. My hand is covering it." He smiled again. "That doesn't mean anything because the moon is like a hundred million miles away from us that's why it looks so small in the first place, plus everybody in the world knows that a hand isn't *bigger* than the moon." "That may be true, but from where we're standing, your hand *can* cover the moon, can't it? And if it *can* cover the moon, that means that it *is* bigger than the moon, doesn't it?" I wanted to say something really smart back to him but I couldn't think of anything and even if I could he would just smile and say something even smarter back to me, so I just agreed with him (which is usually what I did after he asked me one of his questions), put my hand down, got into his car, took out a comic book from my bookbag, and hoped that he wouldn't ask me any other questions during our ride home.

My aunt and uncle lived in this great old house that looked like a small castle made of red and brown bricks and it had a round archway that belonged in a King Arthur story and there were these long green vines that grew on the side of their house and all along the archway and they had this great old wooden door with this great old metal latch and whenever I opened it I kept expecting trumpets to sound and a red carpet to be rolled out for me to walk on.

The first thing you saw when you walked in their house was this really beautiful picture of my cousin hanging on the wall next to this cool old lamp (that also looked like it belonged in a King Arthur story). My cousin must have been around eight or nine years old and she had these perfectly round cheeks and long brown hair that went all the way down her back and her eyes were looking at something that she must have really liked because she looked so calm and happy in the picture.

To the left of the door on this long dresser were all these pictures of my cousins and aunts and uncles, and other relatives and this really cool plant that was over thirty years old. My mother told me that the day my aunt and uncle bought their house they went to Woolworth's to buy some things and my aunt bought five little plants in plastic green containers and when she got back to their house she put all of the plants in this glass bowl and then she put the bowl on the dresser near the window and opened the curtains really wide so that the sun would shine on them all the time and all she ever did was water the plants once a week, that's it, she never moved them or took them out of the bowl or anything, and over the years the plastic containers just fell apart and mixed in with the soil and all five plants turned into one big long flowing beautiful green plant and every time I came over their house I would hold some of the leaves in my hand they felt so smooth and green and fresh and I couldn't believe that five little plants could stay alive for so many years, but the thing that made me the happiest when I slept over was the smell of my aunt's cooking.

When you walked through the front door of her house you could see straight through to the kitchen and the first thing I looked for was my aunt with her apron on moving back and forth from the stove to the refrigerator to the kitchen counter back to the stove then back again to the kitchen counter and I would follow the smell of whatever she was cooking all the way to the kitchen and I would give her a kiss on the cheek hello and she would smile and ask me if I was hungry and I said that I was starving (I used to skip lunch just so I could eat more at dinner), then she would give me a little piece of whatever she was cooking which was usually roast beef because she knew that was my favorite thing to eat but the most important thing that I checked for were the soup bowls. There were six of them whenever I slept over, two for my aunt and uncle, three for my cousins, and one for me and I could tell right away which bowl was mine because it was filled to the top with noodles. My father was Italian (which made me half Italian) and everyone knew how much I liked spaghetti, especially my cousin Robbie, so while the rest of my family had chicken soup with a little noodles in it, I had noodles with a little chicken soup in it, because of her.

After dinner my aunt would bring out this old pink glass jar that belonged to my grandmother and it was filled with her homemade applesauce and let me just say that my aunt's homemade applesauce was the most delicious dessert I ever tasted. She would scoop out portions of it in these pink bowls that she also got from my grandmother and I knew once she put them on the dining room table that meant applesauce was coming and no matter how full I felt I would always make room for a couple of bowls (by loosening my belt buckle and undoing the snap on my dungarees) until I couldn't shove another spoonful in my mouth.

When we were done with dessert, we would all go into the porch, and watch either Perry Mason, Gunsmoke, or Mission Impossible. It's been so long I forgot which one was on Friday night and which one was on Saturday night but it didn't really matter because I didn't pay much attention to what was on tv anyway I just liked being surrounded by my aunt and uncle and cousins as I laid down on the floor right in the middle of them and everywhere I turned my head I saw someone which made me feel so good that sometimes I would fall asleep, right there, on the floor, with the tv playing, and all of them talking which is the best way to fall asleep because it's like I was wrapped up in all of them like a big warm family blanket.

When it was time to go to bed I would go upstairs to my cousin's room which overlooked my uncle's vegetable garden with all of the bright red and orange and green vegetables growing in it and I used to think how cool it was that you could grow your own food in your own backyard and eat it whenever you wanted to and after my cousin showed me his latest invention (about ten years later he actually built his own motor cycle and it really worked) we would fall asleep listening to Bob Dylan or the Beatles and he would let me sleep in his bed while he slept on this old rollout army cot that he brought up from the basement and I can't remember if I ever thanked him for all the times he did that for me but to sleep on this rickety old cot (that sunk to the floor) while someone else was sleeping in your comfortable bed was a pretty cool thing to do. Then sometime later my uncle would sneak into my cousin's room and kiss us both on the cheek and whisper some prayer in our ear and before I knew it, I was asleep.

111

The next morning, I would wake up to the sound of my uncle shaving in the bathroom next to my cousin's room, and I would open the door and there he was his face all covered with shaving cream and he would lean over and kiss me good morning and I would use one of my fingers like it was a razor and scrape off the shaving cream that was left on my face like he did as he whispered, "I'll meet you downstairs," and I would smile and nod my head yes and tip-toe really fast down the stairs and sit on the floor next to my uncle's green leather chair in the porch, and by the time I was all set he'd come in with the newspaper in one hand and a pen and a pencil in the other hand (the pen was for him and the pencil was for me). Then he would sit in his chair and look through the paper until he found it and folded the paper in this special way (he showed me once but I could never do it) and we were ready to start working on the New York Times Sunday crossword puzzle.

When I did the crossword puzzle with my uncle I would usually look for the clues that had blanks in them like "Happy _____ to you." I knew that the missing word was "birthday" and my uncle would let me try and figure out all of the clues I could that had blanks in them while he looked over the crossword puzzle like he was looking over a restaurant menu reading every word then looking at the empty boxes where the answers went then looking at the clues again sometimes the clues that went across and sometimes the clues that went up and down and he told me to always make sure at least two answers fit together up and down and across that way I would know if they were really the right answers because a word could fit in the empty boxes but it may not be the right answer and I told him not to worry the only time I ever did a crossword puzzle was with him and I knew he would check for me. One time the crossword puzzle clue was "sharp object you carry with you," and I screamed out "pocketknife!" and my uncle smiled at me and said are you sure, maybe you should count the empty boxes and see if they match up with your answer and I told him don't worry about it, the answer is right. He said ok and gave me the paper and with my pencil I started putting the letters in the boxes first "p" then "o" then "c" then "k" then "e" and just as I was going to put the "t" in the next box I noticed that there were only four empty boxes left but the word "knife" had five letters in it. I counted the boxes and the letters again, just to be sure, and the word "pocketknife" had eleven letters but there were only ten empty boxes for the answer. I looked up at my uncle who was trying his best not to laugh and after I handed him the paper back and told him that he was right, pocket knife doesn't fit, he said don't worry all we have to do to fix this is add our own extra empty box next to the other ten boxes this way we'll have eleven empty boxes and "pocketknife" will fit just fine. Then he added the extra box with my pencil and started putting in the rest of my answer but I noticed that the extra box stuck out past the end line of the crossword puzzle which didn't look right and I said, "even I know you can't do that," and he said "are you sure" and I said "yeah, I'm sure" then he erased the extra box and after he gave me a few hints I came up with the right word which was "razorblade." After that I just watched as my uncle filled up empty box after empty box with all the right answers until he came to a clue which was just the letter "o" which seemed a little weird to me plus the answer had fifteen letters in it and before I could even guess at an answer my uncle began putting in letters in the empty boxes which spelled out: "s-e-c-o-n-d-i-n-c-o-m-m-a-n-d." At first I didn't understand the answer, then my uncle explained it to me. The letter "o" was the *second* letter in the word "command" that's why the answer was "second in command." After that I just watched Sunday morning cartoons (Courageous Cat and Minute Mouse being my favorite, of course) until my aunt came downstairs and started to make breakfast.

My father died when I was nineteen years old, and for the next thirteen years until my uncle died I would go over his house once a week and my aunt would make us dinner and afterwards we would sit by the kitchen table and do the "during the week" New York Times crossword puzzle and he would still ask me these weird questions only by then I was actually able to answer some of them and I still got excited every time I drove down their block and saw their red brick house with the rounded archway and vines that grew all over the walls, and it makes me kind of sad to write this because I really wish I had someone in my life now who could add a few extra boxes to my puzzle for me when I needed it.

july mornings

I remember most
july mornings
bright blue and clear
and white clouds
still and soft and round
and voices
lots of voices
and laughing

I remember
running through the streets
and laughing

The Weekend

My father lived with my grandmother
in a small, one-bedroom apartment
on a quiet tree-lined street in Maspeth,
Queens. that was usually our first
stop when he picked me up after
school on Friday afternoons before
we would go to the park and then to
the luncheonette on Fresh Pond
Road for a bologna sandwich
and orange soda. and if we got
on the highway by three o'clock,
and if there was no traffic, we could
make it to the park by four o'clock
and get in a few games of handball.

When he drove me home on Sunday
mornings, he would take the streets
from Queens back to Brooklyn.
he said he didn't want to take the
highway because of the traffic, but
that wasn't the real reason. it would take
nearly twice as long to drive me home
when he took the streets, which was
just fine with me, and him too.

He would take 69th Place, where my
grandmother lived, to Grand Avenue
and make a right, then he would take
Grand Avenue all the way down to
Flushing Avenue where the road split,
and take Flushing Avenue for a few
miles until we reached Vanderbilt
Avenue, where he would make a left
and take it to the traffic circle by

Grand Army Plaza. then he would drive about
halfway around the circle until he reached
Prospect Park West. from there he would
drive along the park to a second, smaller
traffic circle, go halfway around that one,
then drive a few more blocks to 20th Street,
which turned into McDonald Avenue after
he made a left turn. he would take that to
Ft. Hamilton Parkway and make a right,
then drive about a mile to New Utrecht
Avenue where he would make a left and
drive under the elevated train tracks until
he reached 50th Street where he would make
another left and take that just over two blocks
to my apartment building, which was just off
the corner of 13th Avenue. and just to be sure
we didn't make the trip back to my apartment
too fast, he would drive under the speed limit
the whole way, something he never did before.

In the summer the trees along the park would grow
so tall their branches would hang down and scrape
the tops of the buses and trucks that drove past us,
while I stared out of the window at the old brick houses
that looked like castles with their black metal gates,
heavy wooden doors, and thick green bushes that were
so tall they covered some of the windows on the front
of the houses. I used to imagine shooting arrows from the
roofs of the houses protecting my castle from the army of
invaders that were trying to capture us. my father would
laugh at the silly shooting noises I would make and it was
usually around this time that I took his big right hand and
held it in my lap and traced the lines of his palm like a map
of the streets, or I would bend his fingers and play them
like the keys to a piano. it was also around this time that it
got pretty quiet in the car because it was only a few more

minutes until he dropped me off and that made both of us pretty sad.

One morning, when I was around eight years old, he stopped his car a few blocks from my building. he was looking in the rearview mirror even though there were no cars behind us. after a few minutes he turned and looked at me. his eyes were red and he took out a handkerchief from his back pocket and wiped them. I could tell he wanted to say something but he just sat there looking at me. I didn't know what to do so I asked him if he was feeling ok. he tried to smile but he couldn't. he pushed away some of the hair from my eyes, and asked me if I had fun with him this weekend. of course I did, I said. I always have fun with you. I started to feel a little scared when he looked away to wipe his eyes again. did I do something wrong? I asked him. if I did, I'm sorry. he laughed. no, you didn't do anything wrong. you never do anything wrong. then he leaned over and kissed me on the cheek. I could hear the plastic of the car seat crackle when he sat back up and started combing his hair. you know, he said, after he took a breath, when you get older you might want to do other things on the weekends instead of spending time with me. you might want to hang out with your friends, or go to a baseball game or watch a movie. you know, things like that. I just sat there looking at his face, his shiny black hair, his white button-down shirt. the sun was coming in through the windows of the car and it made my knees hot. I heard his words but I really didn't understand what he was saying. I didn't know what was going on. I started to say something but the words got stuck somewhere in my throat. I could feel tears rolling down my face. t-t-that's n-never going to happen, I finally said. never. I-I-I'll a-always want to be with you. always. I think about you a-a-all the time. I-I think about d-driving in the car with y-you and going to the p-park w-with you and-and watching tv with you I j-just want to do everything with you.

118

e-e-everything all the time w-w-with y-you. just you. only y-you. I-I always want to be with…he brought me closer to him and hugged me as the rest of my words got lost somewhere in his strong wide chest. I could smell the aftershave on his shirt as I took in breath after breath of him. all I wanted to do was stay right here with him in his car on this street in this spot, right here, with him, just him forever. that's all I wanted to do. that's all I ever wanted to do was to be with him, only him, forever him.

There was a candy store on the corner of my building and after a few minutes he pulled into a spot and bought me a comic book and a big salted pretzel and a chocolate malted. after I was finished drinking the malted, he kissed my forehead and held my hand as we walked back to his car. he opened the door and got inside then rolled down the window and leaned his head outside and I grabbed him around the neck and squeezed him as tight as I could until I had to let go and he kissed me one more time then slowly started driving down the block as I waved goodbye, making a left-hand turn at the corner and then just like that he was gone.

He had to stop driving some years later after he got sick and was forced to move in with my grandmother, but by that time I was old enough to take the train to her apartment by myself to see him. it took just over two hours to get there and in the beginning it didn't bother me that much but after a while it started to get really annoying, especially when it snowed or rained or when the trains were delayed. I could tell he was really happy when I got there by the smile on his face but we really couldn't do much because he was nothing like he once was. he spent most of his days just sitting on the couch, watching tv, playing solitaire, or doing the Jumble in the Daily News. I would tell him about my week and he would smile and nod his head and when I was done, I would just sit there, next to him, on the couch, watching him read the newspaper until my grandmother made us dinner around seven o'clock. by then I would be so bored that after dinner was over I would go for a walk around the neighborhood, which usually took up about an hour. all of the stores were closed and I was too young to go anywhere else, so by about nine I ended up back in my grandmother's apartment, sitting next to him on the couch, watching tv, wishing that I hadn't come to see him and hating myself for feeling like that.

When I was seventeen we started hanging around with these girls from school. it was four of us and three of them, but that didn't matter. we didn't know what we were doing anyway. we just knew that we liked hanging out with girls. we liked the way they laughed, we liked the way they smelled, and we liked the way they would sneak a look at us when we were in class, or when we would walk down the hallway goofing around. by this time I only stayed with him on Saturday nights, then I would leave early Sunday morning, after my grandmother made us breakfast. I would bring my homework and a few books with me, to try and fill up the time, but it really didn't help. and even though I couldn't wait to get out of there I still got teary-eyed when I left.

One Saturday morning before I went to see him, one of my friends came over and said there was going to be a party at one of the girls' houses and we were all invited. you have to come, he said. it's going be great. everybody's going to be there. I can't, I said. I have to go to Queens. can't you miss going there one time. just ONE time? what's going to happen if you don't see him one weekend? he's not going to die. you don't even like going there. Sheila's coming and you know she likes you. I'm sorry. I can't go. I just can't. why not. please. c'mon…just this one time… please…I don't know. I promised him I would come.

so you'll go next weekend. what's the big deal? it's only
one time. come on. I don't know. it's just that, well, he
looks forward to seeing me so much I just can't do that to
him. I just can't...

After my friend left, I finished packing my bag and was
about to leave when I started thinking about the party and
Sheila and everyone who was going to be there and then
I started thinking about sitting on my grandmother's couch
all night watching tv and I started to get mad. then I
thought about taking the train for two hours and how I
wasn't a little kid anymore and that I was eighteen and
eighteen-year-olds don't sit in their grandmother's living
room watching tv with their fathers on a Saturday night
they go to parties with their friends and they have fun and
they make out with girls and things like that and I got even
madder. I put my bag down and just stood in the middle of
the kitchen. I didn't know what to do. I knew what I
wanted to do, but I didn't know if I *could* do it. I finally
picked up the phone and dialed his number. he answered
right away and asked me what time I was coming over. at
first I didn't say anything then I started telling him about
the party and how I liked this girl Sheila and how pretty
she was and that she was going to be there and so were all
of my friends, and that the party was at this girl's house
that we all knew from school and she was really nice and I
kept going on and on until I ran out of things to say so I
stopped talking and waited for him to say something but he
didn't so I took a deep breath and started squeezing the
phone until my fingers turned red and then I asked him if
he would be mad if I didn't see him this weekend and that I
promise I'll come early to see him next weekend and that I
would even stay late on Sunday if he wanted me to it's just
that I really wanted to go to this party and I really wanted
to see him too but I didn't know what to do.

I could hear him on the other end of the phone but he didn't say anything so I asked him if he was ok and after a few seconds he whispered, "I-I'm fine. I'm fine. Go to your party and have a good time. We'll see each other next weekend." I don't know what I said after that I just remember standing there in the middle of the kitchen with the phone in my hand looking out of the window at the bare trees swaying, their branches reminding me of the lines in my father's hands, and I wished that I had never gotten any older.

A Little Older

I was around twelve years old when my mother was let go from her job, and she was really worried about how she was going to support us. I remember making a list of ways in which I thought we could save money until she got another job, as well as how I could take care of her, and my father, so they would never have to worry about anything again. I never actually wrote my mother a letter, but if I had, it would have been something like this.

———————————

Dear Mom,

I heard you crying last night in the kitchen. I'm sorry you feel sad. I know you lost your job last week and you are worried about making enough money for us to live on. I was thinking of a way that we could save money until you got another job. You don't have to cook lamb chops or chicken or the fish that grandma makes for dinner every night for me. I know that costs a lot of money. I can eat what you eat. Cottage cheese, noodles with butter, eggs and toast. I know that eggs are for breakfast but if you can eat them for dinner so can I. We can save money that way. Also, you don't have to buy me Devil Dogs all the time. If you want to buy them I can only eat one at a time that way the box will last longer. I wish I was older than 12. I could get a job and make money so you wouldn't have to worry so much. I know you have to worry about a lot of things because of me. Are you still happy I'm your son? I hope so. I'm very happy that you're my mother. I was also thinking that if I skip 8th grade like my teachers want me to, I could graduate high school when I'm 16. That's only four years from now. That's not a long time at all. Then I could go to college in the morning and work all day after that, even at night if I have to. After college I can get a real job and you won't have to work anymore. You could stay home and take care of your plants. I know how much you like doing that. I like when you cut the leaves off of the long plants I think they're called spider plants and put them in small jars with just water, and you can see the roots of the plants twisting all together like the braids in my cousin Carol's hair. Maybe you could sell them in a store. And if I make enough money maybe we could get a big apartment and my father could live with us too. He's not working either. You don't have to be married to him again. I know you like seeing him when he picks me up for the weekend. He likes seeing you too because you make him laugh so much so maybe it could be like that all the time. You could each have your own room and I could sleep on the couch. I sleep on the couch now and I like it. Please don't worry about things. I will take care of you. I promise I will. I just have to be a little older, that's all.

Thor #36

Back then the trick
was trying to figure out
who would start crying first

My father was pretty slick
he would drop something
on the floor of his car, a pen,
a piece of paper, a nail clipper,
something small
then he would bend down
and make believe
that he was looking for it
under the car seat
or behind the gas pedal
mumbling something under
his breath to make it look good
and when he came back up
he would be wiping his eyes
with his handkerchief
and make up some excuse
that it was hot in the car
or that the fumes from a bus
that passed by a few minutes ago
made his eyes turn red

My mother was pretty slick too
she would open up her purse
and take out her lipstick case
with blue lettering on the front
and a small mirror with a pearl handle on it
and pretend that she was putting on makeup
only every once in a while she would
miss a spot just below her chin

where her tears would fall off
onto her blouse making an oval shape
that she didn't bother to wipe away

And this would go most Sunday afternoons
when he would take me home
and she would be waiting
outside of our apartment building
all dressed up
like she was going out somewhere
only she would tell him
that she was just going to the supermarket
or the drugstore
and ask him for a lift
and then they would both start smiling
when she got into the car
but that never lasted very long

Everything would be ok
for the first few minutes
but then they would start talking
about things I really didn't understand
and their voices would get louder
and their hands would start moving
and then I wouldn't hear anything at all
that's when he would pull over
and shut the car off
and start looking for things
and she would open up her
pocketbook and take out her
lipstick case and small mirror
and I would watch them
not really knowing what to do
trying to get a good look at their faces
but they would always hide them from me
so I started bringing comic books along
so I could hide my face too

This one time I brought along Thor #36
it was the one where Thor lost his hammer
over the Red Ocean of Zarrus
and if he didn't get it back within a day
he would die and he was looking all over for it
as these creatures sent by his evil brother Loki
were trying to kill him and as he was fighting them
he was getting weaker and weaker as they shot
him with deadly rays from the metal claws
that came out of their three eyes

and as I kept reading, I could hear them
from the other side of my comic book
as the pages began to get wet
and I just kept on reading
until he started the car again
and I asked him if he found
his nail clipper and he just
looked at me through the
rearview mirror while she
pressed her face up against
the car window and closed
her lipstick case and put it
back in her pocketbook

Meltdown

I remember being five years old and playing by myself in the living room of our apartment in Brooklyn, trying for hours to sit on top of a big red and white beach ball. I kept sliding off, knocking things over, making a lot of noise, even crying, but neither one of my parents ever came over to help me. I don't know for sure, but I think that's when I started to realize that I was really alone, that I was always going to be alone, and if I wanted to do something, I had to do it by myself, since no one was ever going to be around to help me. When I was thirteen I made the softball team at my sleepaway camp. I was so happy that I made the team, but I was afraid that I wouldn't play well and that I would embarrass myself in front of the whole camp. So the night before our first game, I took two Dramamine (my mother had given them to me so I would fall asleep on the bus and not get sick on the long ride up to camp), and when my counselors tried to wake me up the next morning, I was so groggy I could hardly stand up, so they told me to just go back to sleep, and I ended up missing the entire game. That was the first time I self- medicated (even though I had no idea what the term meant), and realized how sleeping was such a great escape from the pain and anxiety of life. When I was in college, I changed majors so many times that I needed to stay an extra year just to graduate. And even though I was still only twenty-one when I got my degree, I felt like a failure, and from then on, whenever things didn't go the way I planned, or whenever I was having a difficult time doing something, I got in the habit of making myself feel like shit (as some sort of punishment for not living up to the expectations I set for myself), which eventually led back to how stupid and worthless I was because it took me five years to graduate college instead of four.

As I grew older, these ways of thinking became so ingrained in me that by the time I was in my mid-twenties, I had convinced myself that I was better off living alone, because then I would never have to depend on anyone for anything and no one could ever hurt me, that when things got really bad I could always take some kind of over-the-counter medication (like NyQuil or Dramamine) to make me fall asleep and disconnect with the world, and if by chance I was having a good day, I would tell myself that I didn't deserve it, and I would bring up all of the things I should have done in my life but didn't, just to ruin any happiness that I may be experiencing at the time (after all, my parents were never happy, so what right did I have to be happy?).

It took me nearly forty years to realize that this way of thinking was doing me more harm than good, and on those unbearably sad days, I fight as hard as I can not to revert back to them. But it isn't easy. Here is what one of those days looks like.

———————————

I feel it in my ears first. They start to turn red and then get hot. That's the first sign. But it's enough to let me know what's coming next. I start to lose strength in both arms. Sometimes I can't even make a fist with either hand. I try, but my fingers are too weak to squeeze together. They feel brittle and numb, like they could break off at any time. Out of habit I'll shake my arms to try and get the blood flowing through them, but it never does any good. I don't feel anything. It's like shaking out a towel. I might try and rub them, like you do when your leg falls asleep, but that never works either. Nothing ever works when this starts to happen.

Next, my throat gets sore. It's like I'm getting a cold, but I'm really not. When this first started happening to me, I actually thought I was getting sick, until I realized that minutes before this I was feeling fine. My throat becomes so raw and swollen it's almost impossible for me to speak. I can't even drink a glass of water it hurts so much.

But the worst part is the yawning. When the first yawn comes, I hope that I'm really tired, but I know that I'm not, and I know this yawn isn't a good one. By now I can tell the difference. It's too deep and it's too long and my mouth feels like it's made out of sandpaper. The second and third yawns quickly follow. These are much deeper and fuller and it seems as if all of the air is getting sucked out of my body like a balloon with a hole in it. By the fourth yawn, my eye sockets are starting to turn black and it's as if my eyes are receding into the back of my head. Then they start to close. This is it. I'm done. I try to keep my eyes open as long as I can, hoping that if I focus them on something they won't close. That never works. The whole thing takes about ten minutes, from the time I first feel the heat in my ears to the sore throat, the yawning, and then my eyes closing. Most of the strength has left my body. Sleep is not far away. And I absolutely cannot let myself fall asleep. It's like death.

One time when I was driving I actually had to pull over to the side of the highway because I crossed over two lanes and almost hit the guardrail I was so tired. I had no choice but to give in. I fell asleep for almost two hours in some grassy patch that I pulled into so I wouldn't get hit by any of the other cars. It was so bad I almost banged my head on the dashboard I was so groggy. I didn't even have enough strength in my hands to roll up the windows. I tried, but I finally gave up. It hurt too much. It was raining outside when I pulled over. It rained all over me while I was sleeping. I was soaked when I woke up. I felt so ridiculous trying to dry myself off with loose pieces of paper I grabbed out of the glove compartment, still half asleep, the ink running down my shirt and all over my arms. I was so glad no one else was in the car with me. That would have been devastating.

My arms look like they did when I was eight years old. Skinny, weak, no muscle anywhere. I'm so tired I feel like I could sleep for a week straight. But I cannot let myself crawl back into bed and feel my head slowly sink into my pillow and feel the soft, smooth pillow case cover my face as it suffocates me. It's like being lowered into a grave. My head is pounding. My stomach is in knots, throbbing with these little bursts of electricity that feel like broken-off wires sending sparks everywhere. Even my teeth hurt. The yawns are so much deeper now. I pray to God I can muster up enough strength to just stay awake.

I think about going outside and going for a walk. That's what I promised myself I would do the next time this happened. I made that promise when I felt good. When my head was clear and my eyes were round and white and I couldn't possibly imagine feeling like this again. I would never let myself feel like this again, no matter what I said to myself, as if I had a choice, which I don't. But I said it anyway. I always do, hoping that maybe next time it would be different. But it never is.

I have to go outside. I can't put myself through this again. Not so soon after the last episode. I thought everything was ok. I thought I was doing well. Yesterday was such a great day. No headaches. No sore throat. No burning ears. My stomach didn't give me a problem. I was wide awake when I woke up in the morning. My eyes were clear and focused all day. When I went to bed I felt great. It was the third or fourth good day in a row. Then this. Why? Why so soon? WHY SO FUCKIN' SOON? WOULD YOU PLEASE

TELL ME WHY THIS HAPPENED SO FUCKIN'
SOON! I DON'T DESERVE THIS ANY OF THIS!
I sit down on my bed. I pick up one sneaker. I'm so weak I
need both hands to lift up my left leg and lay it across my
right leg. I slip on my sneaker. Tying it is out of the
question. Suddenly I feel a cool breeze on my back. It's
coming from my bedroom window. I turn around and look
outside. It's the middle of May. Such a beautiful time of
year. The sky is water-blue. The trees are moving, dancing.
The sun is reflecting through my bedroom window onto the
top of my dresser. I have a jar full of quarters there, and
they are actually sparkling. The sun is so bright I have to
shield my eyes with my hands because the light hurts them.
Imagine that? The light hurts my eyes. When I was young I
would actually run *into* the light on days like this. Now
look at me. I should be outside enjoying the day instead of
trapped in this self-made furnace, burning from the heat.

I yawn several times in a row. What did I do so wrong that
this is happening to me? Here we go. That old familiar
script starts playing inside my head which makes me feel
even worse. I should be married. I should have kids. I
should have a Ph.D. I should. I should. I fuckin' should.
My head is throbbing. My eyes are almost shut. I can't see
the trees moving outside my window anymore. The breeze
is gone. I'm literally killing myself. I'll never be able to get
out of here. I know it. I'm so tired. I want to go to sleep.
Just for a few minutes, that's all. A few minutes and then
I'll feel better. What's the big deal anyway? Just go to
sleep. Just lean back and get it over with already. Then
you'll feel much better. No I won't. Yes, you will. No, I
won't. I'm not doing it. I'm not going to sleep. IT'S THE
MIDDLE OF THE FUCKIN' DAY YOU FUCKIN'
IDIOT. WHO THE FUCK FALLS ASLEEP IN THE
MIDDLE OF THE FUCKIN' DAY!

I feel so drained. I need a glass of water. I put both hands on my bed and somehow push myself up like an invalid, and stumble to the kitchen. I open the refrigerator and take out a bottle of water. My fingers are so weak it takes me four times to screw off the fuckin' cap. I finish the bottle in one long gulp, water spilling all over me, down my shirt and even reaching my pants. I open the freezer and stick my head inside. It feels so good. So cold. I take an ice cube and rub it on my ears that are still red and burning and the back of my neck. The ice melts so fast. I take another cube and it melts just as fast. I can't keep doing this. Suddenly I start thinking of my mother. Was it like this for her? Was it like this for my father? What did they do when this happened? They must have suffered so much. I know. I saw it. But I was so young I really didn't know the full extent of what they were going through. Besides seeing it and feeling what they felt are two different things. I start to cry. I'm sorry. Why didn't you ever tell me what was going on? I would have helped you. I would have made it better for you. You never gave me the chance. You both died so young. Why did you both have to die so fuckin' young. I would have taken care of you. Why the fuck didn't you ever tell me?

I grab a handful of ice cubes and let them melt down my head and neck. I think of jumping in the shower but if I do that, I'll never leave my apartment. I turn on the cold water in the kitchen sink and splash some water on my face. I feel a little bit better. I gulp down another bottle of water but spit half of it back up I drink it so fast. I don't know what the fuck I'm doing. I'm still yawning but not as much. I wonder what they did when it got bad like this. Did they do anything? Did they even *try* to feel better? In the end he never left the house when I came over to see him, and she only went out to places in the neighborhood that she could walk to. But I'm not like them. I'm stronger than they were. I'm smarter than they were. I understand more about this than they ever did. I won't let this beat me down like it beat them down. I won't let that happen to me. I yawn. Who the fuck do I think I am? He lived through World War II. World War fuckin' II. People were dying all around him. What's the worst thing that ever happened to you? You scraped your knee playing basketball. Poor baby. She was hated by her parents from the moment she was born. Her father hardly ever spoke to her for sixteen years until he died. That's *real* fuckin' pain. Me? I have it so much easier compared to them. A few yawns, my ears get a little red, my throat gets a little sore and I think it's the end of the fuckin' world. Grow the fuck up you weak piece of shit. All you are is a fast-talking, smart-mouthed punk who doesn't know shit about anything. They had it bad. NOT YOU! THEM! THEY HAD NO CHANCE AT A LIFE YOU SELFISH PIECE OF SHIT COMPARING YOURSELF TO THEM. I start pulling at my ears. I want to rip them off my head. I'm all fucked up now. I don't know what to do. If I was married or if I at least had a girlfriend, she would help me. But I don't. I don't have anybody. You wanted it that way, right? Well, you got what you wanted. A few minutes go by. I'm standing in a puddle of water in my kitchen. I'm crying. I wipe my face. Please, please someone help me. Please. I punch myself in the legs like the kids at school do who pull the hair out of their heads, and bite their nails until they bleed when they get so mad they don't know what to do. They don't know why they feel the way they feel and they don't know who to blame, so they blame themselves. What would you say to one of them when they got off the school bus and the look in their eyes tells you they've already been through hell and the day hasn't even started? You'd distract them, make them laugh, break that painful cycle of self-hatred (yes, eight-year-old children really do engage in that painful cycle of self-hatred, and if you don't believe me, just look at the scratch marks up and down their faces and arms when you see them walking in the street or playing in

134

the park) that only makes things worse. You'd tell them that it's only eight o'clock in the morning and they had the whole day ahead of them to feel better. And no matter how bad they felt now, *it wasn't going to be that way forever.* That, you can promise them. And they believed you, because they could tell by the look in your eyes that you spoke from experience. You know that this won't last forever. The only problem is, you don't have anyone to sit you down and tell you that. But you know it's true. So I get up, stumble back to the bedroom, put on my other sneaker, unlock my front door, take the elevator to the lobby, and somehow, because of them, my lovely broken-hearted kids, I make it outside.

The sun is so bright it almost blinds me. I don't know where to go, so I start walking towards the park because it's only a couple of blocks away. I tell myself not to look at anyone, don't give them a reason to laugh at you. Just keep walking. Keep the momentum going. I make it across the street and sit on one of the benches that line the outside of the park. It's under a tree in the shade so the sun won't bother me. I look down at my stomach. It's soft and round. I poke it and it immediately springs back to its original roundness. I do this a couple of times and get madder at myself each time I do it. I feel like a freak. Skinny arms, wobbly legs, and a soft round belly like the Fat Man at a Coney Island sideshow. Suddenly I hear it gurgling. I realize I'm hungry. The thought of eating something makes me sick. But my stomach won't shut up. Shit. I forgot to take any money with me. I reach my hand in my pants pocket anyway and find a five-dollar bill. Thank God. He finally did something nice for me today.

I take a deep breath, pick myself up off of the bench, and walk over to a hot dog stand by the playground and buy two hot dogs and a can of Coke. I'm so hungry I finish the first hot dog in three bites, take a few sips of Coke, then shove the other hot dog in my mouth. I finish the can of Coke. I'm feeling a little bit stronger. My ears don't feel as hot as they did when I first woke up. That's a good sign. On better days I would sit on one of these same benches and either read a book or do some writing. There's this beautiful prewar four-story walkup, The Algonquin, that I usually sit across the street from. It has huge windows, an old wrought iron front door, and is made of beige bricks which you don't see around much anymore. I would always dream about living in one of the apartments in that building and how big and airy the rooms would be and how I would open all of the windows when it would snow outside and feel the coldness of winter coming through and breathe in all of its cold pure freshness. I picture how happy I would be when suddenly from out of nowhere I start yawning again. What the fuck? I notice I'm sweating and my shirt is soaking wet. Maybe I should have stayed inside and turned on the air conditioner. It would have made my apartment nice and cold. It would have also sealed me inside with all the noise it makes and the air blowing all around like you're trapped inside some wind tunnel you can't escape from.

When I was in my twenties I used to turn the air conditioner on high even in the winter to *really* cut myself off from the world. Do that, take some NyQuil, shut the lights off, take the phone off the hook, and a full weekend goes by just like that. The only problem is when Monday morning comes and you feel the same way, what the fuck do you do then? And what about next time this happens? Next time? What about NOW? you asshole. I can't worry about next time. There will be a next time. I know that. But right now, I'm outside. You made it outside. You did it. I force myself to take a deep breath. Then another and another and another. I start squeezing my hands together, and moving my legs up and down. I get up from where

I'm sitting. I start walking. It doesn't matter where I go, the important thing is to just keep moving. I ask someone what time it is. It's a little past one. I still have most of the day ahead of me.

In the Middle of a Dream

I see you walking in line
with the other children
in the schoolyard.

is it really you?
am I really here?
is this really happening?

you look happy.
I don't remember
you being happy.

I want to go over to you.
I want to talk to you.
I've been waiting for this
for so long.

but I'm scared
you won't know who I am.

I can hardly breathe
my chest is heaving.
I'm so nervous.

I take a few steps towards you.
you turn and look at me.
you're smiling.

you know who I am.
I can't believe you know who I am.

I kneel down.
my hands are shaking.
my mind is jumbled, racing.

I cup your face in my hands.
it feels so tender.

I want to tell you so much.
I want you to know it will be ok.
I want you to know it will all be ok.

but I can't speak.
the words have left me.

suddenly, I feel it's *my* face in *your* hands
and *you* are telling *me* that *I* will be ok.

do you know something that I forgot?
what is it? please tell me.
I try but I can't remember.
I need to remember.
I need so much to remember.

I want you to know
I'm sorry for so many things
I didn't do.

please don't be sorry.

don't be sorry?
don't be sorry?

my eyes open.

you're here.
you're still here.

Reconciliation

why didn't you fight it
try harder
do something, anything, instead of giving up
like you did and letting it beat you down
you should have fought harder
when the headaches and dizziness came
and your weak limbs barely held you upright
instead you took the easy way out
you turned off the lights
locked the door and went to sleep
instead of gathering any courage
you had left from all those years of pain and anguish
you both were forced to endure and let it know
that it has no real power over you because it never
really existed it was just a fabrication they
forced down your throat
figuring they could slaughter you
before you even knew who you were

you should have stood up and yelled right
into its decrepit eternal vengeful face to leave you
alone, to leave you and let you live but you didn't
you couldn't? bullshit. the problem was
that you believed what they said about you
you believed their ugly lies they created
to control you, to hurt you, to punish you for crimes
you never committed until it became your own
loveless reality because you were too young
to know any better and you trusted them
to take care of you until it was too late
and its tentacles wrapped themselves
around you squeezing you as you begged
for mercy because you feared it
you let it in, you even nourished it

you let it get to you
you let it diminish you
you let it infiltrate your soul
you let it ruin you

and what excuse did you have? none
you gave up so young
and so easily I saw it
with my own eyes I saw it every day
lying around in your underwear, sleeping
all the time, making up excuses why you couldn't
go outside, go to work, see people at least
be more than just a lump of flesh
flailing around in a sea of hopeless despair
you should have made an effort
to see what your life could have been
like would have been like
but instead you just gave up
all 6'1, 225 pounds of you
big strong Italian man
who fought in the army and came home a hero
who were you kidding? when the real battle came
you laid down your weapons and let it stomp on you
like a burnt-out cigarette the last flicker of life
crushed under some unrelenting image of yourself
that you held up for people to see
and be in awe of while you hid behind it
shaking at the thought of being found out
for the liar you were

I didn't understand it at the time but I felt it
deep inside of me I felt it
I felt all of it the crying the sadness the anger
the wall-punching, the yelling, the screams for mercy
the late nights walking around the apartment mumbling
to yourself, letting the ashes from your cigarettes fall
on the floor (while I followed behind you sweeping

them up afraid you might catch on fire) oblivious
that whoever inflicted so much pain on you
was no longer around to hurt you
but you couldn't let go, you held onto their fantasy
like a blanket made of glass, cutting into you
the further you wrapped yourself inside of it

you thought I'd never find out right?
you thought maybe you could hide it from me
like some private addiction that only affected you
well, I'm here to tell you
you were wrong
I did know what was going on
not with my mind,
but with my sad, shaking, worried, frightened body
torn between wanting to hold you to comfort you and run
away from you because I didn't know what you would do
to me if I let you know that I saw you like that, your bare
raw naked selves if you could cause yourself so much
pain, what could you do to me?

and in the end neither of you could find the strength to
simply put on a coat and go outside and breathe in some
fresh air what was that? was it so difficult?
so elusive, that you couldn't grab hold long enough
to keep yourself from drowning

did you ever think in your isolated, self-involved life
that some little four-year-old boy was watching you,
taking in all of it like spoon-fed morsels he thought he
should ingest because after all you were his whole world
and you were constantly ingesting it so why shouldn't he?
because he wanted, more than anything, to be just like you
and you'll be happy to know that he is

did you ever really notice me?
at any time did you ever really give a fuck about me?
you knew I was there you gave birth to me but
you were so lost in your own miserable world of self-
torture you never realized that I hurt as much as you did
even worse because I never knew what was going on or
why you always stayed away, shut me out, walked right
past me as if I wasn't there
as if I didn't have your blood running through me
however tainted it was
as you barely existed (if you want to call it that) in some
sort of living daze barely alive
hiding behind your masks of
charisma and humor mixed together with that plastic charm
you always displayed, never letting anyone see your real
faces the wounded, morphed faces of constant torment
I wanted to do something but
I had no voice to combat it
to call out to you, "I'm here. I'm here"
I was useless
it was like watching a burning building
holding an empty bucket in my hand
what was I supposed to do?
I was six seven ten twenty years old
it never stopped
but what could I do
if you both did nothing
that's the thing I don't understand
why not fight
why not go right at it
just one time swing away, you were so strong
and you, you were so smart, so aware I know you were
what happened? was it that bad? was it all so bad
that you never even said goodbye
is that why you died so young
so you wouldn't have to explain anything to me
you were my parents

you were supposed to be stronger than me
you were supposed to be around to help me
I lived longer than the both of you, why?
I don't understand any of it

and I hate you for that
for not staying around for me
I stayed around for you but you left me
you never gave me a chance to make any of it better for
you I would have; I'm telling you I would have if you had
just given me a few more years that's all I needed but you
couldn't even give me that
you both were so selfish
you let it destroy you; it destroyed you
chipped away at you bit by agonizing bit
until all I had left was the remembrance
of a mother and father who once were
but who are now just blurry figures
that come into focus when that same despair
descends upon me

and it's only then that I know
just how horrible it was
just how misery tasted
just how much you suffered
just how hard you fought
just how long you lasted
way past anyone
could have ever hoped for

the only one

lying
in a
hospital bed

unaware
of anything
around me

I reach for
the phone
to call you

even though
you've been gone
for so many
years

you're still
the only one

Preface to My Boys

In 1964, I was six years old when I first met a group of
kids that would literally be my lifelong friends. Growing
up in Borough Park, Brooklyn, we did everything together,
from playing every conceivable street game, to eating over
each other's houses, to protecting each other when we
needed it. Then, as is always the case, as the years went by,
we drifted apart, some of us continuing to stay in touch,
while others simply went their own way. That was around
1978. I never stopped thinking about "my boys" or loving
them. I wrote this poem around 2018, as my thoughts kept
bringing me back to them, and our childhood, and the joy
we had simply by being together. Then, a miracle
happened. In 2020, two of my friends got in contact with
each other, then from there more friends were contacted
until one night, nearly sixty years after we first met, we sat
down to dinner (in a diner in New Jersey, of all places),
and despite all that has gone on in our lives, the love that
we have for each other is as strong today, if not stronger,
than it ever was. Barry, Paul, Anthony, Rami, Ronnie,
Joey, Johnny, Alan, Philly (who sadly passed away some
years ago), and Howie: I want you to know that I would
not have made it through my childhood (actually, I would
not have made it, period) without you, and my only wish is
that we stay in each other's lives forever.

My Boys

My boys, My boys, My boys
I listen for the echoes of your voices,
cries in the otherwise stillness of the night
bouncing down hallways and empty staircases
rooftops and alleyways filled with laughter
and hope and the boundless energy of youth
our bodies colliding into one another
sprinkled with the joy and excitement and wonder
of exploring a world yet unknown to us
as we pressed on into the endless void, unafraid,
carried by the unlimited affection for the only
living things that mattered back then: us

My boys, My boys, My boys
where did we go after growing older
and going off to find ourselves lost
now among the years that swept by so
fast we hardly had time to catch
our breaths before adulthood took over
and tried its best to separate us but
in our hearts where it counts the most
it never did

Where are you now? as I call out in the dark night
alone, living a life I chose for myself having no idea of
the consequences that were waiting for me
when I thought it was the only choice I had,
for how could I ever give of myself
wholly, unconditionally, to anyone else but you?

I miss you; do you hear me?
with every ounce of strength I have left I miss you so
that my voice grows hoarse each day, spewing out words
that no one can hear (or wants to hear) except for you

if only I knew you were listening
my only wish is that you are listening

 Do you think of me? do you think of us?
when silent moments creep up on you
early in the morning, as the haze of night
is still etched in your minds and you haven't
yet had the chance to remember
who you are supposed to be so many years later?

Do you ever go back, far back, and allow yourself
the delight of memories, so real and pure that they scare
you for how could such bliss, such joy, such unrelenting
aliveness have ever existed? and how did we ever let it go?
someone please tell me that
why did we ever let it go?

I ask myself, lost in a zombie-like existence,
was it all just a dream that we made up to sooth
ourselves in those years of bewilderment? and
as I stand on our corner after miles of aimless walking
that took me back to where it all started, when our love
for each other held us, protected us, nurtured us,
our belief in each other the only thing that kept us alive
I know, beyond anything else in this world,
it was the truest thing,
you are the truest thing
that I have ever set my eyes upon

My boys, My boys, oh, My boys
what can I do to get you back?
and with it that feeling of aliveness
shown without words
felt without words
understood without the need
to utter even a sound of confirmation to prove its existence
I miss it with every ounce of life I still have left in me

and you, that same ounce of life, unencumbered and
glorious
is it still in you?
is there even a speck left of the cherished moments we
spent together, held in place by a nameless bond we forged
countless years ago?
I know it is.
it has to be.
if nothing else still exists in the world
that has to be…it has to be…

It was there, remember?
as real as the air, as invisible as the breeze
that came swooping down from Heaven
and wrapped itself around us on May afternoons
as we aimlessly ran down block after block around
corner after corner stopping only briefly to catch our
breaths hiding in burnt-out buildings, alleyways, rooftops,
climbing up fire escapes so aptly named because that's
what we were doing escaping from the doldrums of an
otherwise routine existence, that could never quite capture
us, because we had each other, we always had each other

please tell me you haven't forgotten
please tell me you remember as I do.
because if you don't remember
what else is there?
what else do I have left
but the emptiness that this life has to offer me
once filled by you but now?
if it is all untrue
if the feelings that sustained me were simply formed by
my imagination, holograms of a fantasy world I created
to survive the sadness that followed me around
day after agonizing day
then what do I have left but a hollow soul filled
with words and images I found scattered

along the streets we used to roam, words and images
that I gathered together to form a life which was
so much happier than the reality of my own

To run with you, to sing with you, to laugh with you
just one more time and not in memories or dust-covered
pictures or notebooks filled with scribbles of secret hiding
places but now, here, for real, I pray for just one more
glorious time with you, standing on that corner fear and
excitement racing through our bodies
waiting for the light to turn green, fearful of what
might come but knowing with you beside me it will be ok
with you beside me it was ALWAYS ok

My boys, My boys, My boys
I'm telling you now to remind you
in case you've forgotten
look deep inside your soul
it's there, it's all still there
trust me, look, please look
it is all still there, all of it…I promise you
every minute of it, frozen in time,
waiting for us to once again be together

Made in United States
North Haven, CT
02 July 2025

70298138R00094